ON THE PRINCIPLES OF GIBRALTAR TAXATION

ON THE PRINCIPLES OF GIBRALTAR TAXATION

Edited by

Isaac Levy and Grahame Jackson

Assistant Editor

Dr Stephen Noguera

First published September 2024
by Hassans International Law Firm Limited
Madison Building, Midtown, Gibraltar, GX11 1AA
www.spiramus.com

British Library Cataloguing-in-Publication Data.
A catalogue record for this book is available from the British Library.

ISBNs Hardback: 9781913507633
e-book: 9781913507640 Digital

Printed and bound by CPI Group (UK) Ltd, Croydon, CR0 4YY

Gibraltar is neither Spain's to claim nor Britain's to give.
It is the Rock of the Gibraltarians

Sir William Jackson,
The Rock of the Gibraltarians: A History of Gibraltar

CONTENTS

ACKNOWLEDGEMENTS

Many people have helped with this book. Dr Stephen Noguera has been instrumental in the provision of technical input and the supervision of drafts.

Also, Lily Palmer who arranged things and kept people to deadlines and provided general support; and Matthew Baylis who was our professional text editor he was invaluable in turning a series of thoughts into a working text.

Most particularly, though, we would like to thank all those who contributed. This is your work and without you it would not exist. We believe this is the first work of its kind on Gibraltar tax law, and we thank you for making it possible. Gibraltar has a raft of young and talented legal professionals who will take it into the future, and the contributors to this work are most definitely amongst them.

Finally, thank you to all those who put up with proofreading at the weekend, and writing in the evening, the long-suffering family members whose lives have been made a little more difficult by having their loved ones working on this book. Thank you for everything.

TABLE OF CASES

European Union

CJEU

National Courts

TABLE OF LEGISLATION

Australia

China

EU Council Directives (in date order)

Gibraltar

Hong Kong

Kenya

Malaysia

Malta

Netherlands

New Zealand

Singapore

Spain

United Kingdom/Great Britain

United States

TABLE OF INTERNATIONAL INSTRUMENTS

INTRODUCTION

The editors of this book are both partners of Hassans International Law Firm, and both work in the area of tax. With approximately 30 years' experience between us in this field, we have both suffered during our careers from the limited quantity of texts on Gibraltar taxation law (and in fact on Gibraltar law more generally), and that is why we have undertaken to add to the number of works available to practitioners in this area. Prior to the publication of this text, there were only the technical text, Tolley's Taxation in Gibraltar[1], last published in 1999 (and authored by James Levy[2]), and Gibraltar: International Financial Centre,[3] also published by Tolley's, which ran to four editions, the last being the 2006 edition written by Chris White[4]. The editors of this work are grateful to the authors of these previous works, as they have been instrumental in our development as Gibraltar advisers and indispensable as definitive texts. However, we believe there is a space and a need for the creation of a literature which goes beyond textbook-style works (invaluable though they are).

Both in tax law and in life in general, jurisdictions such as Gibraltar require a literature and the open debate that that will encourage. Our connection to the United Kingdom and our legal heritage means that without a literature, much of our law would be simply interpreted through a lens of the English law. Gibraltar law is not English law, though, and whilst the English court's interpretation of similar language is rightly considered highly persuasive, there are many instances where the language of our law differs from that of English law. To ignore those differences would be to undermine the hard-won self-government into which such energy has been, and continues to be invested. If the Gibraltar Parliament makes law which uses different language to that of the United Kingdom, then there is a high probability that it means something different, and as part of the process of interpreting that meaning, we must surely speak and write and have a conversation

1 Levy, J, Kaplan, S Taxation in Gibraltar, Tolley's (1999).

2 Who was then, and still is the senior partner of Hassans.

3 White, CG, Gibraltar: International Finance Centre, Tottel (1996).

4 Who was then tax partner with Hassans.

amongst ourselves. This book is designed to begin a conversation which we hope will lead to a thriving literature in Gibraltar.

In order to maximise the number of voices involved in creating this work, and to maximise the number of people who benefit from the process of writing, we took the decision not to write the work ourselves, but to involve a number of young associates in Hassans. They have worked hard to produce their chapters and the work before you is a credit to their talent and diligence. The quality of their work bodes well for the future of Gibraltar's legal profession.

As we have alluded previously, this is not a textbook. It is instead a series of chapters, each of which describes and discusses a single principle which we believe can be discerned in the design and operation of the Gibraltar taxation system. Not all of these principles will have been in the minds of the drafters of the relevant legislation, some of them may well be what philosophers call 'emergent' properties (that is, they emerge from the system rather than being part of the design of the system), but nonetheless we believe they are there, shaping and guiding the design of new legislation and impacting on the future of our taxation model.

One consequence of this not being a textbook is that the authors can take positions, rather than simply describing fixed law. We fully expect that you may disagree with some of those positions. If you do, we encourage the development of a conversation around what is said, with articles to be published, and debates to be had. Encouraging that conversation is our aim in publishing this book. Finally, in order to further encourage debate, we believe that a journal of peer-reviewed work published once every two years[5], should be established to discuss changes and issues in wider Gibraltar law, and we would welcome such a development, , as a significant step forward in the development of our jurisdiction.

The law upon which we are writing is that law in force as at the 18th December 2023. Tax law develops fast and especially in the years prior to 2023, there have been dizzying levels of international tax reform. We fully expect a second edition of this work will be required in the coming years.

As a final note, of course, nothing in this work should be construed as advice, it is a work of academic endeavour, and advice from a fully competent adviser should be taken on the facts of each case as they are.

5 Similar to the Jersey and Guernsey Law Review.

A Note on History

This work is not the place for a full review of the history of Gibraltar, though that history has been vitally important to the development of the law of Gibraltar. In each of the chapters, you will find references to the relevant history and a short description of the relevant factors. We cannot hope to provide a comprehensive historical overview of the development of Gibraltar, and we are not professional historians, so while we hope that that element is accurate enough to serve its purpose, we humbly remind readers that it is not our main focus.

We also assume a level of knowledge as to the history of Gibraltar, and expect that the average reader of this work will have some understanding of our past. If you do not, there are many fine works on the development of Gibraltar written from a socio-political as well as a simply historical perspective. Suffice to say the history that shaped us goes far beyond the Great Siege and the Royal Navy, important though they are.

Chapter 1

THE TERRITORY IS ALL THAT THERE IS

The Principle of Territoriality

Thomas Blagden and Brian Caetano

Abstract

The principle of territoriality (and by extension, territorial taxation), or taxation based on "source", is a concept well enshrined in international tax law. This chapter examines the historical context behind territorial taxation, and Gibraltar's rationale for adopting this system of taxation instead of a system of worldwide taxation, such as the one employed by the USA. This chapter will show that territorial taxation diminishes double taxation, avoids double non-taxation and facilitates transparent tax competition, and that despite early criticisms, territorial taxation systems have grown in popularity over the course of the 21st century.

Introduction

A feature of today's economy is that individual states must consider to what extent, if at all, they are prepared to tax profits. Broadly speaking, a state may elect to implement legislation to pursue either of the following systems of taxation or a combination:

(i) a company or person resident in its jurisdiction should pay tax on the profits which it earns worldwide (referred to throughout this chapter as worldwide taxation); or
(ii) a company or person resident in its jurisdiction should only pay tax from such profits as are accrued and derived in its jurisdiction (referred to throughout the rest of this chapter as territorial taxation).

Gibraltar has a system which is, at its core, a territorial system such as that at (ii); in this chapter we will explore the reasons why such a system is suitable and preferable for Gibraltar, and we will discuss the implications of such a system.

The taxing of the global income and gains of a resident of a jurisdiction can be argued to be a system which facilitates tax justice between the resident of the jurisdiction and the jurisdiction itself; that is, that there is no favouring of those that have foreign income over those that have purely domestic income. It is, practically, the case that those who are wealthier are more likely to have foreign income. It is therefore, no surprise that a number of large and powerful states with internationally connected economies have historically taxed on a worldwide basis; the most obvious examples being the USA and China.[6]

The alternative method of simply taxing that economic activity which occurs within the territory of the jurisdiction appears to be an intrinsically fairer system when considering the interaction between states. It allocates taxing rights dependent on the tangible reality of economic activity, instead of the artificial construct of residence. Territorial taxation is a form of taxation well suited to operate amongst states which are closely economically integrated, such as those in the European Union, or those forming part of the former British empire.

As territorial taxation systems are simpler to administer, they do not require an assessment of worldwide income and gains, and complex issues such as permanent establishments are not relevant to the calculation of taxation. Since the person or entity in question merely submits a return for their jurisdiction relevant income, it will come as no surprise that 'smaller' jurisdictions have traditionally favoured territorial taxation systems, as they free them of the concern over income which they may not have the capacity or facility to properly asses. Small territories do not have extensive treaty networks or other mechanisms to facilitate assessment of worldwide income and gains.

It follows logically from the above that Gibraltar implemented a territorial taxation system, with s. 11(1) ITA reading as follows:

---

6 In recent years many of the global economies have moved away from a worldwide basis to a *de facto* territorial basis of taxation (even if in form they have a *de jure* worldwide base) see Matheson, T. *et al Territorial vs. Worldwide Corporate Taxation: Implications for Developing Countries, International Monetary Fund* (2013). In this chapter we are not discussing this kind of *de facto* territoriality but instead the *de jure* type implemented in Gibraltar which has no backstop 'worldwide' style provisions.

> 'Tax shall, subject to the provisions of [the ITA] and of the Rules, be payable at the rate or rates specified from time to time for each year of assessment or accounting period upon the income specified in tables A to C inclusive of Schedule 1 accruing in or derived from Gibraltar of any person.'[7]

Gibraltar's adoption of a territorial regime in the ITA in 2010 was not a departure, the ITA was entirely consistent in its approach to territoriality with the ITA52 (the only previous income tax provision in Gibraltar) and the ITA52 had its roots in the earliest iterations of taxation systems for British overseas territories.

The Gibraltar system has suffered some criticism, both from the European Union and from tax campaigners. However, the position of the Gibraltar Government, the Gibraltar tax authorities, and the UK Government[8] is that the administrative simplicity of the territorial system means that it is the only method which a jurisdiction of such a small size can feasibly adopt. Territorial systems were once the exception amongst developed jurisdictions but in recent years this has changed. Gibraltar is now part of a growing number of countries to have adopted a territorial tax system (whether de jure or de facto). As of 2014, 28 of the 34 OECD member countries had adopted territorial tax systems or provisions which resembled such systems, with major developed countries such as New Zealand, Norway, Japan and the UK having all switched to a form of territorial taxation system in the past decades.[9]

Historical context

First Iterations of Income Tax

The first iteration of what would become income tax in Great Britain was conceived as a temporary wartime measure by William Pitt the Younger, to service

7 Income Tax Act 2011, s 11(1)

8 Commission Decision (EU) 2019/700 of 19 December 2018 on the State Aid SA.34914 (2013/C) implemented by the United Kingdom as regards the Gibraltar Corporate Income Tax Regime (notified under document C(2018) 7848) C/2018/7848.

9 Supra Note 6

the growing national debt and the spiralling costs of the Napoleonic Wars.[10] It was implemented in 1799. The underpinning sentiment was egalitarian: such a tax on income would apply to all those with income over a certain level, no account would be made of birth or status. Although its results were disappointing, it paved the way for a tax on 10% of income, which would be imposed the following year.[11]

What followed was a stop-start period, where income tax was repealed in 1802 following the declaration of peace, revived again in 1803 on the resumption of war, and then abandoned in 1816. In 1842 Sir Robert Peel restored the income tax, under which tax would be payable on all income from property in Great Britain belonging to British subjects (whether resident or not) and on the income of all persons resident in Great Britain. Broadly speaking, three groups were liable to tax on their income: all persons in Great Britain upon all their income, whatever its source; non-resident British subjects upon income arising from property in Great Britain, and any body politic or body corporate, and any company, fraternity or society of persons (whether corporate or non-corporate) on its income in Great Britain.[12]

Although outside the scope of this chapter, it is worth mentioning in passing just how little the substance of the operative provisions of the above have changed when compared to the United Kingdom Income Tax Act 2007. The income tax in the United Kingdom is, for example, still an annual tax which must be renewed every year.

Dependant Territory Territorial Taxation

The framework set out by Pitt, Addington, and Sir Robert Peel formed the basis and justification for which taxes were levied upon colonies in support of Great Britain. This taxation took the form of poll tax, income tax and import duties, and as settlers accounted for a very small portion of the population in the colonies,

---

10 An Act to Repeal the Duties Imposed by an Act, Made in the Last Session of Parliament for Granting an Aid and Contribution for the Prosecution of the War, and to Make More Effectual Provision for the Like Purpose, by Granting Certain Duties Upon Income, in Lieu of the Said Duties 1799 (39 GEO III c 13).

11 Alzada Comstock, 'British Income Tax Reform', The American Economic Review [1920], pp. 488, 489

12 https://www.att.org.uk/history-income-tax-and-hmrc (Last accessed on 26th February 2024)

the tax burden fell on the local population.[13] This permitted exploitation of the colonial economic base by enterprises located in the home country and with a limited tax base for their own resources.

Towards the end of the British empire when Britain's position was shifting, beginning in the inter-war period and accelerating after the Second World War, there was a shift in the administration of British colonial rule over its dependant territories, with a view to the colonial states becoming financially self-sustaining.[14] This break from the extractive regime would require a rethink of dependant territory taxation rules, as the local populations began to be considered more widely, the colonial territories would require greater resources. It was against this background that a Royal Commission sought thoroughly to overhaul the British Empire's inter-jurisdictional income tax system. The Commission's report recommended that the British Parliament take certain steps to prevent burdensome tax duplication between Great Britain and the Dominions and Colonies, wherein an individual might be subject to taxation at source in the colony and also taxation in the home territory of the person in question; this remains a conundrum in spite of many efforts, most particularly the over 3000 double taxation treaties currently in force[15]. This can be seen as the first attempt by a multi-national global empire to institute a rational system of taxation which protected the interest of all its constituent parts.[16]

Following the recommendations of the Commission, an Inter-Departmental Committee on Income Tax was formed to consider the problems raised by

13 Pachai, Bridglal, 'Taxation.' In *Colonialism: An International Social, Cultural and Political Encyclopedia* [2003], pp.574, 575

14 Ewout Frankema, 'Raising revenue in the British Empire, 1870-1940: how 'extractive' were colonial taxes?' [2010] pp.447, 445

15 Brian J Arnold 'An Introduction to tax treaties', *International Tax Primer*, Wolters Kluwer (2016)

16 The late 19th Century did see a similar development amongst the German states (see Hattingh, Johann, 'On the Origins of Model Tax Conventions: 19th Century German Tax Treaties and Laws Concerned with the avoidance of Double Taxation' (January 1, 2013). Studies in the History of Tax Law, vol 6, J. Tiley ed, (Hart: Oxford 2013), 31-79 but this British attempt at a multi-jurisdictional system would be of much wider global reach.

imposition of tax in colonies not possessing responsible government,[17] and its report was subsequently published in 1922.[18]

In assessing the viability of a worldwide taxation system, the Committee decided that the complications and difficulties which necessarily accompanied such a system of taxation were so great that, in the special circumstances of comparatively small jurisdictions, it was in the best interests of non-self governing colonies and jurisdictions to limit the scope of an income tax charge solely to that income which would arise in the relevant territory.[19]

The conclusions of the Report were that the most appropriate taxation scheme for dependant territories was one which imposed tax upon income which either had its origins in the colony, or whilst originating outside the colony, was received in the colony,[20] i.e., a territorial taxation policy. The Committee's reasoning for this conclusion was three-fold:

(i) such a taxation system would avoid the various administrative difficulties inherent in an income tax code under which taxation rates varied depending on whether an individual was resident or non-resident,
(ii) it would reduce the problems arising out of double-taxation of income to comparatively small jurisdictions, and
(iii) it would promote uniformity across the dependent territories, leading to greater certainty as to the taxation rights of each jurisdiction.

The recommendation which followed was that dependant territories should, where possible, adopt a form of the model ordinance annexed to the report.[21] The operative provision of the model ordinance reads as follows: 'Income tax shall... be payable... upon the income of any person accruing in, derived from, or received

---

17 John MacArthur Maguire, 'Relief from Double Taxation' [1923] pp. 769, 770

18 Great British Inter-Departmental Committee on Income Tax, *Report of the Inter-Departmental Committee on Income Tax in the Colonies not Possessing Responsible Government* (1922)

19 *Ibid*, para 10

20 *Ibid*, para 9

21 The model ordinance was based closely on the Income Tax Act 1918 of the UK, see OOI, Vincent. Tax law. (2021). Law and technology: The practice and content of law in Singapore. 451-473. 7

in, the colony....'[22] This sets the basis for a territorial taxation system in the British overseas territories, and the foundation upon which Gibraltar's current taxation system is built.

Although the territorial scope of the model ordinance was limited to the then British empire, it is worth noting that the model ordinance's provisions dealing with double taxation between colonies, and between colonies and dominions, produced the same result as the double taxation provisions between the taxing colony and the United Kingdom.[23] This is an example of an early precursor of the promotion of effective tax cooperation between different jurisdictions with territorial taxation systems in place.

Adoption of the model ordinance

Notwithstanding the Committee's recommendations to establish territorial taxation systems, it is useful to examine the extent and effectiveness with which the model ordinance was implemented across the former empire.

Singapore

S. 10(1) of the Singapore Income Tax Act provides for income tax to be payable for each year of assessment on the income of any person which accrues in, is derived from Singapore, or is remitted to Singapore.[24] Therefore, in line with the recommendations of the committee, income in Singapore is taxable only if it is sourced in Singapore.

Malaysia

Similarly, tax residents in Malaysia are taxed on income accruing in, derived from, or received in Malaysia, even if it is from an outside source.[25]

Hong Kong

Somewhat differently to the two above-cited examples, s.14 of Hong Kong's Inland Revenue Ordinance reads 'arising in or derived from Hong Kong',[26] removing the

22 *Ibid*, Appendix 1

23 *Ibid*, paras 41, 59 - 60, Annex 1

24 Income Tax Act (Ch.134) 1947, s 10(1)

25 Income Tax Act (Act 53) 1967, s 3

26 Inland Revenue Ordinance (CAP 112), s 14

remittance wording included in the model ordinance.

The Hong Kong legislature had initially considered adopting the words 'received in', as suggested by the Draft Income Tax Ordinance 1961, but ultimately decided to adhere solely to the 'accrued and derived principle', to avoid establishing a worldwide taxation system. The Financial Secretary of Hong Kong at the time, Sir John Cowperthwaite, argued that Hong Kong 'should continue to refrain from taxing overseas income... [Hong Kong] should in any case have to give most of it back under double taxation agreements... this would make it rather less difficult to prevent evasion than now'.[27]

Malta

A review of the Maltese Income Tax will show that the underpinning legislation which has been much amended is the Model Ordinance, s4 particularly is in a very similar format and language to the model ordinance and would be very familiar to a practitioner in Gibraltar, despite its many subsequent amendments. The slightly modified phrase 'accruing in or derived from Malta' and variations thereupon litter the act, the ancestry of which is very clear.[28]

Kenya

Almost identical wording can be found in s. 3(1) of the Kenya Income Tax Act, which reads '...income tax shall be charged for each year of income upon the income of a person... which accrued in or was derived from Kenya'.[29]

Gibraltar

To reflect Gibraltar's growing self-governance and need for its own resources, the Gibraltar Legislative Council was established in 1950, and tasked by Great Britain with introducing a modest tax assessed on trading profits, to be paid by local trades and businesses.[30] To this end, the Income Tax Act 1952 was enacted, borrowing heavily from the drafting of the 1922 model ordinance. The main taxing provision in the 1952 Act read as follows: 'tax shall... be payable... upon the income of any

---

27 *Ibid* 165

28 Income Tax Act s4

29 Income Tax Act (Cap. 470), s 3(1)

30 HC Deb 26 April 1950, vol 474 cols 934-935

person accruing in, derived from, or received in, Gibraltar...',[31] deploying exactly the same wording as the 1922 model ordinance, and establishing a territorial taxation system in Gibraltar.

The 1952 Act was eventually repealed and replaced by the Income Tax Act 2010, which confirmed the territorial taxation for companies. The language of the operative provisions was adapted slightly to bring it more in line with the established territorial taxation systems of Kenya and Hong Kong, with the operative provisions now reading as follows:

> "Tax shall, subject to the provisions of this Act and of the Rules, be payable at the rate or rates specified from time to time for each year of assessment or accounting period upon the income specified in tables A to C inclusive of Schedule 1 accruing in or derived from Gibraltar of any person."[32]

> "Tax shall, subject to the provisions of this Act and of the Rules, be payable at the rate or rates specified from time to time for each year of assessment upon the income specified in table B and table C of Schedule 1 accruing in, derived from or received in any place other than Gibraltar of any person ordinarily resident in Gibraltar other than a company."[33]

Conclusion

Far from being novel, Gibraltar's current territorial taxation system can trace its roots back to the very conception of income tax. Much like other former overseas territories of the British empire, the foundations of Gibraltar's taxation system are based on the recommendations of the Committee Report and its annexed model ordinance. Therefore, Gibraltar's territorial taxation system is not an outlier, but rather is based on sound historical and widely applied principles. Territorial systems which may appear to be divergent from the 'norm' of taxation to those who have spent their life within an expansive system which utilises the League of Nations Residence/source[34] type model are not outliers or aberrations but instead

31 Income Tax Act 1952, s 6(1) (repealed)

32 Income Tax Act 2010, s 11(1)

33 *Ibid*, s 11(2)

34 See the League of Nations Committee of Experts, Double Taxation and Tax Evasion (1925) League of Nations

a long-standing solution to the problems of small jurisdictions, a tradition within which Gibraltar squarely sits.

The Meaning of 'Accrued and Derived'

Having analysed the historical basis on which Gibraltar's current territorial taxation system is based, it remains to examine exactly what would fall within the territorial scope of the 2010 Act, and whether it achieves the intended aim of establishing a territorial taxation system.

The Income Tax Act 2010

As a starting point, 'accrued and derived' is defined within the 2010 Act itself, as follows:

' "Accrued in and derived from" shall –

(a) be defined by reference to the location of the activities which give rise to the profits;

(b) for the purpose of (a), the activities which give rise to the profits of the business shall be deemed to take place in Gibraltar in the case of –

  (i) a business whose underlying activity that results in the income requires a licence and regulation under any law of Gibraltar; or

  (ii) a business which can lawfully be transacted in Gibraltar, through a branch or any form of permanent establishment, by virtue of the fact that it is licensed in another jurisdiction which enjoys passporting rights into Gibraltar and which would otherwise require such licence and regulation in Gibraltar;

(c) subsection (b) shall not apply to any branch or permanent establishment of a Gibraltar company undertaking activities outside Gibraltar to the extent of the activities conducted outside Gibraltar;'.

As originally enacted, s. 74 of the 2010 Act referred to the preponderance of activities, leading to some ambiguity as to when an activity would be caught by the above definition, and an intimation that Gibraltar would monitor the worldwide income of a company. This wording was deleted by the Income Tax (Amendment) Regulations 2013, removing any uncertainty as to the intended territorial scope of the 2010 Act.

The intention of the legislator was clearly therefore to create a territorial taxation system.

Interpretation by the Income Tax Office

Basic rule

For its part, the Income Tax Office has laid out the basic rule that, in deciding whether profits of any person accrue in and are derived from Gibraltar, it will look at what the person has done, or proposes to do, to earn the profits in question, and where the person has done it, or intends to do it.[35] The focus is therefore on establishing the geographical location where the activity and the relevant profit-producing transactions took place. Regarding the provision of services by a company, the Income Tax Office has indicated that it would rely on the geographical location at which all the income-generating activities (and not simply the back-office or administrative support functions) take place, in order to determine where the services giving rise to fees are performed.[36]

In determining whether an activity would be caught by the basic rule, the Income Tax Office applies the principles derived from Hang Seng[37] and HK-TVB,[38] which it has accepted as being authoritative in Gibraltar, in accordance with the general provisions of Gibraltar law.[39] The United Kingdom in its submissions to the European Union argued that even though decisions of the Judicial Committee

35 HM Government of Gibraltar, Commissioner of Income Tax, *Guidance on Accrued and Derived* (2018) para 20

36 'Procedures Relating to the Implementation of the Competition Policy, European Commission: State Aid- United Kingdom', available online on: https://eur-lex.europa.eu/legal-content/EN/TXT/PDF/?uri=CELEX:52023AS34914 (Last accessed on 26th February 2024)

37 *Commissioner of Inland Revenue v Hang Seng Bank Ltd* [1990] S.T.C. 733, [1991] 1 AC 306

38 *Commissioner of Inland Revenue v HK-TVB International Limited* [1992] S.T.C. 723, [1992] 2 AC 397

39 HM Government of Gibraltar, Commissioner of Income Tax, *Guidance on Accrued and Derived* (2018) para 21

of the Privy Council concerning jurisdictions other than Gibraltar are not binding in Gibraltar, they may be relied upon by the Gibraltar courts because of the similarity of the legislation in the two jurisdictions.[40]

Hang Seng

In its assessment of the basic rule, the Income Tax Office notes that in Hang Seng a subtle distinction was drawn between profits of a trade carried on in the jurisdiction and profits arising in or deriving from the jurisdiction. It therefore follows that profits from trade carried on by a taxpayer in Gibraltar might have arisen in or accrued from different sources, from Gibraltar or not. Only those that arise in or derive from Gibraltar are taxable in Gibraltar.

Additionally, it was held that the question as to where profits arose in or derived from would always be dependent on the nature of the transaction. In his judgment, Lord Bridge summarised: 'the broad guiding principle, advocated on the attestation of many authorities, is that one looks to see what the taxpayer has done to earn the profits in question'.[41]

In respect of trading profits, where the purchase contract or the contract of sale takes place in Gibraltar, the Income Tax Office follows the judgment of the court in *Magna Industrial Co*,[42] which considered the locality of trading profits against the guiding principles set out in Hang Seng. Following the judgment, the initial presumption of the Income Tax Office is that such profits will be fully taxable in Gibraltar.

The focus is therefore on establishing the geographical location of the activity that produced the profit for the transaction, and not the activities which are antecedent or incidental to those transactions. This requires an accurate factual analysis of the transaction. For example, it was maintained in Hang Seng that the fact that investment decisions were being made in the taxpayer's resident country

40 Official Journal of the European Union, 'Procedures Relating to the Implementation of the Competition Policy, European Commission: State Aid- United Kingdom' (2023/C52/02), available online on https://eur-lex.europa.eu/legal-content/EN/TXT/PDF/?uri=CELEX:52023AS34914, (Last accessed on 26th February 2024)

41 *Commissioner of Inland Revenue v Hang Seng Bank Ltd* [1990] S.T.C. 733, [1991] 1 AC 306

42 *Commissioner of Inland Revenue v Magna Industrial Co Ltd* [1996] 3 HKC 210, [1997] HKLRD 171

does not necessarily mean the profits were accrued and derived in that same country. In his judgment, Lord Bridge provided the following guidance on the application of this rule in practice:

> 'if the [taxpayer] rendered a service or engaged in an activity such as the manufacture of goods, the profit will have arisen or derived from the place where the service was rendered or the profit-making activity carried on. But if the profit was earned by the exploitation of property assets, as by letting property, lending money or dealing in commodities or securities by buying and selling at a profit, the profit will have arisen in or derived from the place where the property was let, the money was lent or the contracts of purchase and sale were effected'.[43]

HK-TVB

HK-TVB expanded the guiding principle set out in Hang Seng to 'look[s] to see what the taxpayer has done to earn the profit in question and where he has done it'.[44] The approach to be taken, therefore, in determining whether profits have accrued or derived in Gibraltar, is to ascertain which operations produced the relevant profits, and where those operations took place.

To illustrate the above point, following the judgement in HK-TVB, where any goods are manufactured in Gibraltar, the profits arising from the sale of such goods will be fully taxable in Gibraltar, since the profit-making activities are the manufacturing operations carried out in Gibraltar. If a company manufactures goods outside of Gibraltar, but sells them through a branch in Gibraltar, then only the profits attributable to the Gibraltar branch will be taxable in Gibraltar.

Conclusion

Both the drafting of the 2010 Act and the relevant case law successfully apply a territorial taxation regime. The relevant case law (and in addition the interpretation applied by the Income Tax Office through its guidance) is entirely consistent with the original principles of the 2010 Act. As the taxation systems in both Gibraltar and Hong Kong are based on the same recommendations of the committee

43 *Commissioner of Inland Revenue v Hang Seng Bank Ltd* 1990] STC 733.

44 *Commissioner of Inland Revenue v HK-TVB International Limited* [1992] S.T.C. 723, [1992] 2 AC 397

report and annexed model ordinance, the Gibraltar court (and therefore both the Income Tax Office and the practitioner when advising their client) is entitled to rely on Hong Kong case law to guide its interpretation of territorial taxation provisions. This approach of seeking to rely on cases from within the British overseas territories reinforces the international and inter-jurisdictional approach which was taken by the original drafters of the model ordinance. The Gibraltar taxation system remains part of a global system of courts and precedent and as a result exhibits a robustness which would be lacking in a system implemented entirely in isolation by such a small jurisdiction.

Continuing Rationale for Gibraltar's Territorial Tax system

Having assessed both the historical justification for Gibraltar's territorial taxation system, and the application of its principles, we must now consider why Gibraltar continues to implement such a system.

The arguments consistently advanced in favour of territorial taxation argue that it is a powerful force for the promotion of fairness within a tax system. The concept of fairness will be considered in this chapter in relation to four elements, namely: (i) the source of income and residence; (ii) double taxation; (iii) double non-taxation and simplicity, and (iv) tax competition.

Before exploring each of the heads set out above, it is pertinent at this juncture to expand on the brief description of a territorial taxation system given at the beginning of the Chapter. In international tax, territorial taxation is generally understood to refer to something more limited than the concept of respect for territorial boundaries. The International Bureau of Fiscal Documentation's International Tax Glossary defined the 'Territoriality Principle' as follows:

> 'Term used to connote the principle of levying tax only within the territorial jurisdiction of a sovereign tax authority or country. The underlying theory is that no taxes can be levied outside this area without violating the sovereign tax authority of another state. Consequently, both residents and non-residents of a state adopting this principle are only taxed on the income from sources in that country and properly situated in that country...'[45]

---

45 Barry Larking ed., *IBFD International Tax Glossary* (revised 5th edn, 2005) p 414

Although not dealt with at length in this chapter, the above is clearly indicative that the taxation of 'territoriality' is strongly linked to the source of income.

The source of income and residence

The importance of source and residence as a criteria on which to base taxability has been discussed at length, giving rise to important publications from organisations such as the International Fiscal Association (See, for example: Cahiers de droit fiscal international, vol 90a (2005) Source and Residence: new configuration of their principles). The contributions contained in the IFA recognise that the source doctrine, and therefore the concept of territoriality, are well-enshrined in tax systems around the world. For example, in their General Report to the IFA in vol 90a, Angel Schindel and Adolfo Atchabahian state:

> 'Whereas most developed – capital-exporting – countries apply the residence or domicile jurisdictional principle (nationality in the USA) in the name of horizontal equity, capital importing countries, in general, continued to apply the source principle in exercising their natural taxing powers on events taking place with their territory, while strengthening the revenue-raising potential of the tax.

Yet this is not an "either/or" issue. Countries with residence – or nationality-based taxation also apply the source principle on local income derived by non-resident or non-domiciled recipients'.[46]

In addition to ensuring fairness between states, the territoriality principle also advances fairness between taxpayers in the state in which the profit arises. To put this another way, territoriality advances capital import neutrality (see Chapter 4 for a wider discussion of the principles at play here). This is also noted by Schindel and Atchabahian:

> 'The exclusive application of source-based taxation requires that foreign income from residence country taxation. Thus the source principle is best suited to meet [Capital Import Neutrality] since it applies the same tax rate whether income is derived by a resident or non-resident of such country. In

46 Angel Schindel and Adolfo Atchabahian, *Cahiers de droit fiscal international* (2005) p 25

> other words, the tax system should not affect the competitive position of companies, regardless of their nationality. Every investor, whether local or foreign, should achieve the same after-tax rate of return'.[47]

Double-taxation and fairness

Double taxation arises where comparable taxes are imposed in two or more states on the same taxpayer in respect of the same taxable income or capital, e.g. where income is taxable in the source country and in the country of residence of the recipient of such income. Double taxation takes the form of either: (i) juridical (the same person being taxed twice on the same income by more than one state), or (ii) economic (more than one person being taxed twice on the same item).

As discussed earlier in this Chapter, the issue of colonial double taxation was addressed briefly in the Committee's Report, which set out that the issue of double taxation had been exhaustively considered by a sub-committee appointed by the Royal Commission, the conclusions of which had been accepted without reservation, and which were as follows:

> 'Firstly, that in respect of income taxed both in the United Kingdom and in a Dominion, in substitution for the existing partial reliefs there should be deducted from the appropriate rate of the United Kingdom Income Tax (including Super-tax), the whole of the rate of the Dominion Income Tax charged in respect of the same income, subject to the limitation that in no case should the maximum rate of relief given by the United Kingdom exceed one-half of the rate of the United Kingdom Income Tax (including Super-Tax) to which the individual taxpayer might be liable; and

Secondly, that any further relief necessary in order to confer on the taxpayer relief amounting in all to the lower of the two taxes (United Kingdom and Dominion), should be given by the Dominion concerned.'[48]

The committee seemed simply concerned with juridical double taxation and for the remainder of this chapter it is juridical double taxation that we shall refer to when we use the phrase 'double taxation'.

---

47 *Ibid*, p 35

48 Report of the Inter-departmental Committee on Income Tax in the Colonies not possessing responsible government, His Majesty's Stationery Office (1922)

In their report to the International Fiscal Association in 2011, Gauthier Blanluet and Phillipe J. Durand draw attention to the fact that territoriality and the doctrine of source are concepts strongly linked to double taxation, stating:

> 'It is common to hear that the tax world is divided into two separate groups of countries. The first group includes countries which implement a worldwide taxation system, whereby residents are taxed on all their income, including their foreign source income. The other group comprises countries which have adopted a territorial system of taxation, which basically means that they tax business income only if it is derived from sources within the country.
>
> In principle, countries taxing income on territorial basis do not have to worry about international double taxation. Foreign source income being exempt in the country of residence, taxation can only be levied by the country of source. In contrast, countries taxing income on a worldwide basis have to deal with potential double taxation. This is because while the income is taxed in the country of residence, it is also almost inevitably taxed in the country of source'.[49]

As Blanluet and Durand say, countries taxing income on a territorial basis do not have to concern themselves with double taxation.

Indeed, were source taxation to be employed by all states, double taxation could only arise to the extent that either they disputed the right to control each other's territory (as a matter of EU law, Gibraltar is not a territory subject to disputes over its control),[50] or they had different definitions of source. The latter can arise, as Holmes has pointed out where, for example, the income produced by a ship may be regarded as having its source in (i) the place of loading or embarkation, or (ii) the territorial waters it traverses.[51] But it is true, nevertheless, that double taxation is a much less significant problem where source taxation is used. This fact has made source taxation attractive to policy makers creating closely associated groups of

---

49 Blanluet and Durand, *Cahiers de droit fiscal: key practical issues to eliminate double taxation of business income* (2011) p 20

50 *European Commission (C-106/09 P) and Kingdom of Spain (C-107/09 P) v Government of Gibraltar and United Kingdom of Great Britain and Northern Ireland*

51 K. Holmes, *International Tax Policy and Double Tax Treaties: An Introduction to Principles and Application* (2007) p 23

states. The CARICOM double tax agreement of 1994 and the Andean Pact are said both to rely upon source taxation rather than residence taxation.[52] In relation to the CARICOM agreement, it has been said that:

> 'The unique feature of this multilateral DTA is that it is premised on exclusivity of the source state's right to tax and prohibition against the taxpayer's state of residence levying tax on a worldwide income basis (at least in respect of income derived from other treaty partner states). On this basis, double taxation does not arise… thus obviating the need for an article in the DTA to relieve the impost of juridical double taxation.' [53]

Source taxation has obvious advantages not just for CARICOM and the Andean Pact, but also for the European Union. If all European Union Member States gave full effect to the territoriality principle, then the double taxation of the profits of corporations would not be a major problem. The fact that it endures as a major problem can be seen from the European Commission's Communication, 'Double Taxation in the Single Market'.[54]

Therefore, territoriality is frequently achieved using appropriate provisions in double tax treaties. One country, amongst others, which appears to take this route is Spain (which is explored in further detail below).[55] Such a course is not open to Gibraltar, it has no or very few resources with which to build an effective network of treaties, and as a result is bound by practicalities to take the more transparent approach of securing the principle of territoriality through its primary domestic legislation.

---

52 R. Rohatgi, *Basic International Taxation, Vol 1, Principles of International Taxation* (2018) p 76

53 See K. Holmes, *International Tax Policy and Double Tax Treaties: An Introduction to Principles and Application* (2007), p64, IBFD]

54 Communication from the Commission to the European Parliament, the Council and the European Economic and Social Committee 'Double Taxation in the Single Market' COM (2011) 712

55 Supra Note 1

Double non-taxation, fairness and simplicity

Conversely to double taxation, double non-taxation arises from a failure to improperly allocate taxation rights between jurisdictions. An inevitable consequence of the dual taxation systems of residence and source is that it allows for exploitation and creates an imbalance in the burden of taxation rights. Algidas Semeta, Commissioner for Taxation, Customs, Anti-fraud and Audit agrees saying on 29th February 2012 that '[t]ackling double non-taxation will… ensure a stronger, fairer Single Market for all EU businesses'.[56] If all taxation systems were to adopt taxation at source, then the risk of double non-taxation would be greatly reduced, as there would be no lacuna with regard to the allocation of taxation rights.[57]

The use of a territorial taxation system therefore not only avoids double taxation, but also avoids double non-taxation. If profits arise, or have their source, in one of two or more countries, each of which impose territorial taxation, then it is likely to follow that only one of the countries will have taxing rights in respect of the profits (Double non-taxation is a matter on which TAXUD concluded consultation on 30th May 2012). There can be no failure to allocate taxing rights as may arise where states employ a worldwide taxation system. Such a system depends, for example, on the application of complicated rules for determining corporate residence which are unnecessary where source taxation is employed. It follows from this that the territorial approach to taxation ensures administrative simplicity. There is no need for any mutual agreement between states' tax authorities because their taxing rights are defined by reference to their established, and internationally recognised, boundaries.

Administrative simplicity is a matter to which the Ruding Committee, set up by the European Commission in 1990, referred in its report in March 1992. Although it notes some disadvantages to source taxation, it also stated clearly that:

> '…national tax authorities probably find it more difficult to levy taxes on activities undertaken in other Member States. Hence, source-based taxes are

56 European Commission – Press Release, 29th February 2012

57 Though administratively this would create many challenges globally, not least the harmonisation of the meaning of the word "source" or "accrued in and derived from" across in excess of 200 jurisdictions.

easier to administer than residence-based taxes'.[58]

Gibraltar's use of a territorial system of taxation is, therefore, very much driven by the need for administrative simplicity. It is not enough to have a tax system; a jurisdiction must have a functioning tax administration. It goes without saying that administrative simplicity and fairness are also inextricably linked. The former is often a necessary requirement for the latter.

Territoriality and tax competition

The existence of tax competition within the EU has long been judicially acknowledged. For example, Léger AG has said: 'It may be regrettable that competition operates between the Member States in this field without restriction. That is, however, a political matter'.[59]

The European Commission has made its position clear in the now moribund[60] Proposal for a Directive on the CCCTB, which stated that: 'Fair competition on tax rates is to be encouraged.' [61] The principle of territoriality facilitates open, fair and transparent competition, in which fiscal liabilities and tax rates are easily identified and not obscured by a variety of exemptions and reliefs.

EU Challenges

Notwithstanding the rationale underpinning Gibraltar's choice of a territorial taxation system, the European Commission has examined the territorial tax regime in Gibraltar; although this is through the context of State Aid,[62] it is helpful to examine the commentary in respect of the applicable 'reference system'[63] i.e., the ordinary or 'normal' tax system applicable to the Member State Concerned.

In the arguments advanced by the UK in respect of passive interest and royalty tax exemption, it was argued that the non-taxation of foreign-source passive

58 Report of the Committee of Independent Experts on Company Taxation (1992) p 41

59 Case C-196/04 *Cadbury Schweppes plc* [2006] ECR I-7995, para 55

60 At the time of writing the EU was in the process of replacing the CCCTB with the BEFIT proposal, however, it seems the Commission's position is unchanged.

61 Proposal for a Council Directive on the CCCTB, (2011) p 4

62 State Aid SA.34914 (2013/C) implemented by the United Kingdom as regards the Gibraltar Corporate Income Tax Regime

63 Case C-374/17 *Finanzamt B v A-Brauerei* [2018] para 36

interest is the logical consequence of the territoriality principle, which is based on the aim of avoiding double taxation. Secondly, it was argued that the exemption for Gibraltar-source interest and royalties is justified by the logic of any tax system considering the cost of collection must not exceed expected revenue.[64] In its comments, Gibraltar supported the arguments made by the United Kingdom and stated that if the exemptions were found to be selective, these were justified by the logic and general nature of the system as a consequence of the territoriality principle. Gibraltar further pointed out that the exemption for passive interest and royalty income is justified by concerns about administrative manageability, since costs associated with the collection of the tax are expected to be larger than the actual tax yields.[65]

The Commission accepted the arguments submitted by Gibraltar and the United Kingdom and agreed that defining the ITA as the 'reference framework' was in line with the European Court's case law, which had consistently held that the reference system to be considered was the corporate income tax system of the Member State in question which applied to undertakings in general, and not the specific provisions of that system applicable only to certain taxpayers or certain transactions. For instance, in *World Duty Free Group*,[66] a case concerning the rules governing investments in shareholdings, the European Court endorsed the European Commission's position that the reference system was the Spanish corporate income tax system, and not the specific rules governing the tax treatment of those investments.[67]

In the absence of any other relevant provisions, this is an acceptance of Gibraltar's territorial system by the European Commission.

Conclusion

Gibraltar ′s territorial taxation system continues to promote fairness and promote healthy tax competition. Gibraltar has implemented the system which best benefits its specific needs, and whilst it may not conform with the 'standard' system based on a combination of taxing rights arising from residence and source,

64 *Ibid,* para 52(6)

65 *Ibid*, para 55

66 Joined Cases C-20/15 P and C-21/15 P *Commission v World Duty Free Group, Banco Santander SA, Santusa Holding SL*, para 91

67 *Ibid*, Para. 92

it is not an unfair system. As highlighted, a universally adopted territorial scheme may well lead to an elimination of tax avoidance which exploits the artificiality of the provisions of the League of Nations model perpetuated in the OECD Model Convention.[68]

Is there a territorial system for individuals?

The tax system imposed on individuals ordinarily resident in Gibraltar is stated in Section 11 of the 2010 Act. For our purposes, the relevant clauses are s.11(1) and s.11(2), which read as follows:

> 11(1) – tax shall, subject to the provisions of this Act and of the Rules, be payable at the rate or rates specified from time to time for each year of assessment or accounting period upon the income specified in Tables A to C inclusive of Schedule 1 accruing in or derived from Gibraltar of any person.
>
> (2) – tax shall, subject to the provisions of this Act and of the Rules, be payable at the rate or rates specified from time to time for each year of assessment upon the income specified in Table B and Table C of Schedule 1 accruing in, derived from or received in any place other than Gibraltar of any person ordinarily resident in Gibraltar other than a company.

These subsections, when combined, create the charge to tax in respect of individuals ordinarily resident in Gibraltar. As can be seen from the above, the first limb creates the territorial scope ('accruing in or derived from Gibraltar of any person'), whilst the second limb creates the global charge ('accruing in, derived from or received in any place other than Gibraltar of any person ordinarily resident in Gibraltar other than a company'). As such, the income specified in Table A is only taxable where it has accrued in or derived from Gibraltar.

As discussed above, corporate bodies are taxed in Gibraltar by way of a territorial form of taxation. Despite the above seeming to suggest that individuals are taxed on a global basis, we will demonstrate that the principles underpinning the taxation of corporate bodies and the principles underpinning the 1922 Model

68 OECD, 'Model Tax Convention on Income and on Capital', (OECD, 2017)

Ordinance largely extend to individuals ordinarily resident in Gibraltar. This in turn gives rise to a single regime of taxation that covers all entities and individuals in Gibraltar (except Cat 2 qualifying individuals).

The income specified in Table A (involving a territorial charge) is as follows:

(1) The profits or gains of a company, a foundation or a trust from any trade, business, profession or vocation, and
(2) Any rents, premiums and any other profits arising from any interest in real property.

Where (1) above is an entity-centric provision that is taken to include all profits or gains of corporate bodies arising out of the business of that body, (2) is an all-encompassing provision (insofar as that it is not limited to entities but also includes individuals), that includes rents, premiums and other profits derived from an interest in property.

With regards to s.11 (2), the income specified in Tables B and C which result in a Gibraltar charge to tax for a Gibraltar resident, irrespective of whether that income has accrued in, derived from or been received in Gibraltar, include:

1. The profits and gains from employment and self-employment;
2. Dividends;
3. Inter-company loan interest;
4. Funds income;
5. Income from rights (in respect of dividends, inter-company loan interest or funds income);
6. Royalties;
7. Income from movable property;
8. Pension, charge or annuity income;
9. Sweeping up class (anti-avoidance provision), and
10. State aid recovery.

S.11(2) of the 2010 Act seems to suggest that Gibraltar subjects its residents to tax on their worldwide income, irrespective of the location of the source from which the income is derived.

Despite the above being the general position with regards to income earned by ordinary Gibraltar residents, Table B of Schedule 1 of the 2010 Act outlines a different position in respect of Gibraltar residents who are in self-employment. Here the 2010 Act carves out a position whereby the profits or gains arising out of self-employment are charged on a territorial basis, thus meaning that if the entirety of the activity is carried on outside of Gibraltar, there will be no Gibraltar charge to tax. However, where there is any activity related to trade performed within Gibraltar, Table B (2) (b) sets out that 'such a trade, business, profession or vocation shall be treated as indivisible and any activities of a similar trade, business, profession or vocation carried out in another country, territory or jurisdiction by an ordinarily resident individual either in self-employment or as a member of a partnership... shall be regarded as part of the Gibraltar activities'. We can therefore see that, where the self-employment involves any trade-related activity being carried out in Gibraltar, the entirety of the operation will be liable to a Gibraltar tax, irrespective of the jurisdiction within which the rest of the operation is undertaken.

When compared to the provisions covering those in ordinary employment, this provides a contrast in the form of the language used, despite arriving at a similar conclusion. Table (B) (1) considers the position in respect of those in employment and sets out that the profits or gains from any office or employment, shall be liable to be charged to tax. Here there is no mention of or importance given to the location in which the employment is carried out. Despite this seeming to create a global aspect to the charge to tax of ordinary Gibraltar residents, it in fact reinforces the territorial dimension, under the doctrine that employment is inextricably tied to the individual. Despite the wording of the relevant section seeming to create a global charge, upon review and consideration we can see that it in fact gives rise to a territorial charge.

As such, under the principles of Gibraltar tax law as outlined by the 2010 Act, the employment of an individual, where they are employed by a third party who remunerates them for the work done, cannot be separated from the individual. The individual and their employment are intrinsically and inextricably linked, irrespective of the jurisdiction within which their employment occurs. The mere fact of being an ordinary Gibraltar resident in the course of employment is sufficient for a charge to tax in respect of the income received by the ordinary Gibraltar resident.

Another example of a type of income that creates a question as to its taxability is 'income from property' as outlined in Schedule 1, Table A (2) of the 2010 Act. This, as previously mentioned includes 'any rents, premiums and any other profits arising from any interest in real property'. However, as per s.11(1) and (2) of the 2010 Act, the income specified in table A is only charged where the income described has accrued in or derived from Gibraltar. As such, rental income received by a Gibraltar resident is only taxed where the income-generating property itself is located in Gibraltar. Therefore, any rental income or premium in respect of property, received by an ordinary Gibraltar resident arising from property located outside Gibraltar will not be liable to a charge to tax by the Gibraltar tax authorities. This is a further example of a Gibraltar resident being taxed on a territorial basis.

Another instance where the ordinary Gibraltar resident is liable to a charge to tax in respect only of income arising in Gibraltar— thus exhibiting a territorial charge as opposed to a global charge — is illustrated in respect of the charge on dividends received by the Gibraltar resident, as outlined in Table C, Class 1 (a). Here, as we recall, s.11 (2) suggested that all income of the form specified in Tables B and C will be subject to a charge to tax when received by a Gibraltar resident, irrespective of where that income has been generated. However, upon inspection of Table C and its provisions, it becomes clear that this is not the blanket position in respect of all the income specified in these Tables.

Given that the position as per s.11 is that all income specified in Table C will be chargeable to tax, Table C, Class 1 (a) imposes the following exceptions:

(a) 'Dividends except dividends paid or payable-
 - (i) by a company to another company;
 - (ii) to a person who for the purposes of this 2010 Act is not ordinarily resident in Gibraltar;
 - (ii) by a company the shares of which are listed on a Recognised Stock Exchange;
 - (iv) out of profits or gains on which no tax has been charged in accordance with the provisions of this 2010 Act to the extent that the amount of the dividend represents the distribution of such profits or gains,

and for the purposes of this paragraph, "a Recognised Stock Exchange" means any stock exchange, regulated market or equivalent body as the Commissioner designates to be a Recognised Stock Exchange by Notice in the Gazette.'

The first three of the above exceptions are specific. However, it is the exception found at (iv) that changes the charge to tax on dividends for Gibraltarian residents from being a charge on a global basis to being a charge on a territorial basis. This is as a result of the wording used in (iv) above.

The exception at (iv) creates an exemption wherein any profits which are not liable to a charge to tax as per the provisions of the 2010 Act, will not be charged to the extent that the funds distributed by way of dividend were not chargeable to tax initially. In this, as per s.11 (1), any profits of a company are only chargeable where they have accrued in or derived from Gibraltar (territorial test), thus meaning that profits that have accrued in or derived from outside Gibraltar will not be chargeable to tax in Gibraltar. As such, all profits of a company that accrue and derive from outside Gibraltar will not be chargeable to tax in accordance with the provisions of the 2010 Act. Therefore, where a Gibraltar resident receives dividends from a company that has generated the income to be distributed from a location outside of Gibraltar, the dividend received by the Gibraltar individual will not be chargeable to tax. This once again exemplifies the territorial approach that has been employed by Gibraltar and the Gibraltarian Tax Authorities.

Conclusion

The answer to the question 'is there a territorial system for individuals?' must, therefore, be 'Yes', at least in modified form. It is not as clear-cut, nor as comprehensive as that for companies; some of the forms of language appear to tax in a global manner but when considered in the round, the taxation provisions applicable to individuals do mean that there are circumstances where they will be taxed simply on their Gibraltar-sourced income. The original form of the 1922 Model Ordinance, which has occupied so much of our time in this chapter, made no distinction between individuals and companies or other kinds of taxpayers. There is a logic to this, but it is flawed. If one takes the approach to the heads of charge taken in Schedule 1 of the 2010 Act, then there needs to be a distinction between companies and individuals; it is just always the case that a company cannot be 'employed' or 'self-employed', and therefore applying Table B to companies makes no sense.

It is not clear to us why the drafters of the 2010 Act chose to embed a form of territoriality for individuals in the heads of charge (such as with Table B and its carve-out for trades and professions, none of the elements of which are performed in Gibraltar) and not in the provisions of s11, as it is for companies. It may be that it was for simple drafting reasons, or possibly presentational reasons, or because they preferred to grant an exemption from such income in the Heads of Charge rather than excluding such income from the tax base altogether, or possibly that they wished to tighten the test for territoriality over and above the 'accrued and derived' language which is so much a part of the DNA of the 2010 Act.

What we do know is that the common understanding of a sharp division between the taxing of individuals and of companies is far from an accurate portrayal of the position. It is more nuanced and intellectually consistent than that misunderstanding allows.

A Principle Modified

In recent years the principle of territoriality has been modified and necessity requires that we detail the most important development with regards to the evolution of the Gibraltarian tax system. This centres around the entry into force of the 2010 Act, and the various rulings by the EU Commission and the recommendations by the EU Code of Conduct (Business Taxation) Group (the 'EUCCG') in that respect. When the 2010 Act was first introduced, it did not include any provisions governing the taxation of passive income. The charge to royalties and non-trade interest as found in the 1952 Act had been removed. However, given that any liability under these would arise only where the income was 'accrued in and derived from' Gibraltar, the fiscal impact of the removal of this charge was minimal. This was because they were generally considered ineffective charges.

There are two main documents which impact on domestic tax policy with the EU at a Union level. The first is Article 107 of the Treaty on the Functioning of the European Union, which is commonly called the State Aid article and secondly the Code of Conduct on Business Taxation (CCBT) the CCBT, as created by ECOFIN in 1997, is not a legally binding instrument, but rather it disposes of a strong political force. This is exemplified in a speech given by Lord Bethell in the House of Lords during the run-up to the creation of the CCBT, in which he stated:

> 'The noble Lord, Lord Bethell, also raised questions relating to EU tax harmonisation. The tax code is part of a package of tax harmonisation measures currently under discussion by member states and will take the form of voluntary, non-statutory and non-binding political agreements. It is at this stage too early to say what its effect will be on Gibraltar because negotiations

on the code are continuing in Brussels.'[69]

The Member State's implementation of the CCBT is monitored by the EUCCG which is a group chaired by the European Commission, that pools together the tax authorities of the EU Member States and whose function is to regulate any new tax measures imposed by Member States and to require amendment to any laws or practices deemed to be contrary to the principles or criteria of the EUCCG.The criteria set out are as follows:

- an effective level of taxation which is significantly lower than the general level of taxation in the country concerned;
- tax benefits reserved for non-residents;
- tax incentives for activities which are isolated from the domestic economy and therefore have no impact on the national tax base;
- granting of tax advantages even in the absence of any real economic activity;
- a basis of profit determination for companies in a multinational group which departs from internationally accepted rules, in particular those approved by the OECD; and
- a lack of transparency.[70]

As discussed by Sir Peter Caruana, who was the Chief Minister of Gibraltar during the initial creation of the 2010 Act, the fiscal consequence of removing the taxability of such forms of income was negligible in respect of the effect on Gibraltar's public finances:

> 'there was some lobbying for the complete removal of the charge on interest from the profession, mainly because a more aggressive charge would make several existing businesses unviable and the charge as it was drafted was moribund. There was very little tax loss to the government as a result of its

69 Hansard House of Lords, 'Hansard 26 November 1997' (*UK Parliament website*, 26 November 1997) available online on: https://publications.parliament.uk/pa/ld199798/ldhansrd/vo971126/text/71126-05.htm (Last accessed on 26th February 2024)

70 https://www.consilium.europa.eu/en/council-eu/preparatory-bodies/code-conduct-group/ (Last accessed on 26th February 2024)

removal.'[71]

This change, as presented by the 2010 Act in respect of passive income was seen by the EUCCG as a 'harmful tax measure'[72] given that, in their view it conflicted with the principles and criteria that they had set down. It was also attacked by the EU Commission as unlawful state aid[73].

It was as a result of the ongoing Commission process and pressure from the EUCCG that, on the 1st of July 2013, the Government of Gibraltar (HMGOG) introduced provisions under Schedule 1, Table C (creating a new, Class 1A) which gave rise to the taxation of 'inter-company loan interest' and on the 1st January 2014 introduced further provisions under the same Table which created a charge to tax in respect of royalty income. These amending provisions provided as follows:

Class 1A

'Inter-company loan interest'

(a) subject to (b) below, interest paid or payable by a company to another company arising from a loan or advance between these companies.

(a) For the purposes of (a) no interest is chargeable where-

(i) the interest received or receivable from any one company is less than £100,000 per annum; or

(ii) the interest constitutes a trading receipt as defined by Schedule 3 paragraph 15 and is taxed accordingly.

For the purposes of (a) and (b)-

(i) interest will be deemed to accrue and derive in Gibraltar where the company in receipt of the interest is a company registered in Gibraltar; and

(ii) for the purposes of determining whether the threshold in (b)(i) has been exceeded, interest received from different

71 Sir Peter Caruana in interview 27th November 2019 – in Grahame Jackson, 'From Outcast to Acceptance' (unpublished), [2020]

72 Press release HMGOG 24th June 2013 Microsoft Word - 441.doc (gibraltar.gov.gi)

73 Commission Decision (EU) 2019/700 available online on: https://eur-lex.europa.eu/eli/dec/2019/700/oj (Last accessed on 26th February 2024).

companies will be considered to be from the same company where such companies are connected persons, as defined in paragraph 9 of Schedule 4.

Class 3A
'Royalties'

(a) Subject to (b) below, royalties received or receivable by a company.
(b) For the purposes of (a) royalties will be deemed to accrue and derive in Gibraltar where the company in receipt of the royalty is a company registered in Gibraltar.

These are the provisions that were introduced as a result of the conclusions of the EU Commission.

As can be seen from these provisions, the new Class 1A charge created a four-limbed test for interest income:

a) there must be interest;
b) the interest must be in excess of £100,000 per loan, or an aggregate of loans between related parties (as defined in paragraph 9 of Schedule 4 of the 2010 Act);
c) the interest must be 'paid or payable' by one company to another company;
d) the interest must arise from a loan between those companies, and
e) if the Company receiving the interest is registered in Gibraltar the interest is deemed to have accrued and derived in Gibraltar. 74

The last limb of this test, which looks at the place of registration of the company to decide where the income was accrued in and derived from, undermines the territorial principle in that it no longer looks to where the income was deemed to be generated. However, this only applies to registered entities. The general principle of territoriality continues to subsist underneath. Therefore, if a foreign company has interest income which meets the multifactorial test laid out in *National Bank of Greece SA v Westminster Bank Executor & Trustee Co (Channel Islands)* [1971]

74 Grahame Jackson, 'From Outcast to Acceptance' (unpublished), (2020) p.62

AC 945 in favour of Gibraltar as the source of the interest income, then it may be argued that that interest income would be taxable regardless of registration (as it would be 'accrued in and derived from' Gibraltar and is 'income specified in tables A to C' as per s11(1) of the 2010 Act[75])

It is interesting to realise that it is only in the case of a company 'registered' in Gibraltar that this deeming provision is relevant; in a sense, it restrains itself to the boundaries of the territory even here. It is only those companies that have sufficient legal substance to be considered 'Gibraltarian' rather than simply resident that will be subject to this deeming provision, an act of subjection to Gibraltarian authority in the form of a registration is required to apply this rule.

Similarly, for the chargeability to tax of royalties, as per Table C, Class 3A (b), for the income to be deemed for the purposes of the 2010 Act as having accrued in and derived from Gibraltar, the company in receipt of the royalties must be registered in Gibraltar.

Thus, the form if not the principle of territoriality is preserved. Territoriality is so central to the taxation system of Gibraltar that it must have been unthinkable to the drafters of the 2013 amendments to contemplate a rule which created a standalone charge; instead they worked within the intellectual framework which already existed.

Conclusion

Territoriality remains at the core of the taxation system of Gibraltar. No aspect of the system's design can be clearer to us. One may well consider there to be a spectrum of territoriality, ranging from the purest form in the taxation of companies in trade, through the taxation of individuals, to the purely formal deeming provision which modifies the principle of territoriality but only for those companies within the territory. Territoriality is all-pervasive and even when the tax system is reformed, it remains central at least to the thinking of the drafters.

75 S11(1) Income Tax Act 2010

Chapter 2

A LOCAL TAX FOR LOCAL PEOPLE

The Principle of Difference for Different Persons

T Rahmany and C Oppenheimer

This chapter explores the historical development of Gibraltar's population and the challenges faced by small jurisdictions in managing and taxing their diverse populations fairly. It examines the unique demographic evolution of Gibraltar by tracing historical events, including territorial disputes and migrations, delving into the challenges arising on account of the high degree of economic and practical reliance on cross-border workers. As a result of the challenges posed by this shifting and dynamic population, Gibraltar has developed a three-tier tax system which categorises the tax-paying population into three broad sectors: those who sleep in Gibraltar, those who sleep in Spain, and non-residents whose presence and economic activities in Gibraltar render them liable to taxation.

This chapter will analyse the three-tier tax system, by giving an outline of the Allowances Based System (ABS) and Gross Income Based System (GIBS), which offer tax benefits to residents. The chapter will also examine the difference in tax rates and allowances applied to resident and non-resident individuals.

Lastly, alternative taxation regimes are also explored, focusing on High-Net-Worth Individuals (HNWI) who may wish to apply for Category 2 status and High Executives Possessing Specialist Skills (HEPSS) status depending on their personal circumstances. These regimes are designed to attract non-resident individuals wishing to invest in Gibraltar, as well as highly skilled professionals whose presence would benefit the jurisdiction by contributing to its economic growth. The chapter concludes by comparing these schemes with other residency-by-investment programs available globally and emphasises Gibraltar's commitment to international tax information exchange.

Introduction

The development of Gibraltar's population

Throughout its history, Gibraltar's population has undergone significant changes. By exploring key events, such as territorial shifts, migrations and political and economic factors, we can seek to gain a deeper understanding of its demographic evolution through immigration and the emergence of the cross-border worker.

Without a doubt, Gibraltar's strategic location at the entrance of the Mediterranean Sea coupled with its relative lack of resources has led to its development as a trading hub. In the 19th century, Gibraltar became an important refuelling station for ships and a centre for maritime trade. In turn, this economic growth resulted in inward migration, attracting a diverse array of individuals, including merchants, labourers and skilled workers, particularly from Malta and Italy, resulting in a population surge. The prosperity brought about by trade and the British military presence created employment opportunities and fostered population growth. Malta — also part of the British Empire — had a large number of coal workers, and, with the increasing Royal Navy presence and modernisation of the fleet, job opportunities for coal heavers arose in Gibraltar, which were available to Maltese residents by virtue of their shared British status. Generally, Malta, like Gibraltar, depended economically on Imperial Britain's interests, which meant that employment supporting the British armed forces, such as in Gibraltar's Royal Dockyard, offered attractive prospects and many Maltese had directly transferrable skills.[76]

Gibraltar's multi-cultural and religiously tolerant society also meant that immigrant Jews, Genoese, Maltese and Indian workers all came to call Gibraltar home (a Jewish community has been present on the Rock since the British captured it in 1704, thus making it one of the longest-standing communities in Gibraltar). The common factor these groups shared was commerce, as well as a shared relationship with a colonial influence, as described immediately above.[77]

---

76 Henry Frendo, 'The Gibraltar-Malta Nexus: Two European Mediterranean Identities in Onetime Fortress Ports' available online on: https://www.um.edu.mt/library/oar/bitstream/123456789/24832/1/HF-The%20Gibraltar-Malta%20Nexus.pdf (Last accessed on 26th February 2024)

77 Dominique Searle, 'The San Roque Talk' *Cuadernos de Gibraltar- Gibraltar Reports* (January- December 2015)

Throughout the Second World War, Gibraltar played a vital role for the Allied forces, as a strategic stronghold to the entrance of the Mediterranean. As thousands of British military personnel were stationed on the Rock, Gibraltar's population grew.

Despite several attacks on Gibraltar, no significant damage was caused. After the war, however, Spain's claims to the territory were revived by General Francisco Franco, and the sovereignty dispute escalated, leading to the closure by Spain of its physical land border with Gibraltar between 1969 and 1985, and the severance of transport and communications links with the territory. The sovereignty claim persists to date, albeit this is outside the scope of this present piece.

The partial reopening of the land frontier to Spanish and Gibraltarian pedestrians in December 1982, was followed by the full reopening of this to motor vehicles in February 1985, in preparation for Spain joining the European Communities the following year. This period also coincided with the closure of the Naval Dockyard in 1985 and the gradual running-down of the miliary establishment. Whilst many British personnel had remained in Gibraltar after the Second World War, thus contributing to its population growth, the closure of the Naval Dockyard had a dramatic impact on the workforce. The economic shockwaves were demonstrable in the 1991 census, being the first conducted in Gibraltar after the re-opening of the frontier. The census results demonstrate that there were a total of 1,730 cross-border workers out of a total labour force of 14,040. This meant that 12.3% of the total labour force was commuting to Gibraltar from Spain.[78] Just 12 years later, the total number of employees was recorded at 15,419, of which 2,862 were cross-border workers, amounting to 18.5%.[79] By 2022, the increased reliance on cross-frontier workers was even starker — there were 18,179 employee jobs with 8,944 of them (over 49%) carried out by cross-border workers.[80]

In recent decades, Gibraltar's population has experienced steady growth due to various factors. Gibraltar's status as a financial centre and its low-tax environment have attracted international businesses, resulting in an influx of professionals seeking employment. Gibraltar is largely self-governed, with its own legislature and executive government, although the United Kingdom retains responsibility

78 Census of Gibraltar 1991, p. 11 and 12

79 Government of Gibraltar, 'Employment Survey Report, October 2003'

80 Government of Gibraltar, Statistics Office 'Employment Survey Report, 2022'

for international relations and defence.[81] This has allowed for the development of a favourable tax regime, the establishment of a robust educational system and healthcare infrastructure, making Gibraltar an attractive place to live and raise families in. Such factors, along with increased tourism, have contributed to population growth and demographic diversification.

Challenges of managing the population in small jurisdictions

Gibraltar is a small jurisdiction, heavily dependent on a cross-border workforce, and as such faces certain economic vulnerabilities. Fluctuations in the labour market, changing immigration policies and shifting political priorities can disrupt the stability of the workforce, leading to labour shortages or oversupply and impacting on the growth of the local economy.

If they are to be accommodated in Gibraltar, the influx of foreign workers can place a strain upon public services, including healthcare, education, and housing. If they are to be accommodated outside the jurisdiction, then inadequate travel infrastructure for daily commutes can lead to congestion, increased commuting times, and a reduced overall quality of life for both residents and cross-border workers, as well as leaving Gibraltar vulnerable to pressure on its land border.

The only plausible way to address these challenges requires a mixed solution involving comprehensive planning, investment in infrastructure, and policies that promote integration and social cohesion. Small jurisdictions must strike a delicate balance between leveraging the benefits of cross-border workers while ensuring the long-term sustainability and well-being of both the local population and the cross-border workforce. In other words, Gibraltar cannot simply become a central business district for La Linea de la Concepcion with its workers using La Linea as a dormitory town, but it also cannot hope to provide continued economic growth by retaining an isolationist approach. It must tread a path between these two poles.

The contrast in size between Gibraltar and the surrounding Campo area, coupled with an open border creates lasting opportunities for cross-border integration which in turn, offers an ability for both sides of the border to grow. This makes it possible to increase the flow of people and goods and drive economic growth for all by easing administrative friction to allow economic realities to be the dominant factor in play as opposed to the difficulties created by passports,

---

81 Gibraltar Timeline 'A brief history of Gibraltar' < http://gibraltartimeline.com/brief-history-of-gibraltar/> accessed 15th July 2023

customs and the like. In particular it means that certain industries or services which require greater space (such as industrial manufacturing, waste disposal and agriculture) can be de-localised whilst remaining sufficiently proximate for the local population to benefit or profit from them.[82]

However, in order to balance this outward-looking approach the Governments of Gibraltar have been conscious of the unique characteristics of the Gibraltarian populace and have all taken steps to preserve the unique national character which has resulted from the immigration and integration described above. It is true that the Government of Gibraltar is a government of the Gibraltarians who make up the vast majority of the registered voters of Gibraltar, and whose special status is preserved by the Gibraltarian Status Act 1962, and that Gibraltarians have an interest in the preservation of Gibraltar as a separate jurisdiction. It is also true that the obligation of the Gibraltar Government is solely to Gibraltar. It should not implement taxation policy in a scatter-gun approach which would have effect both at home and across the border. For example, if it wished to encourage the Gibraltar property market there is an argument that it should do so without allowing similar incentives for those investing outside Gibraltar. This was the effect of the taxation system prior to the introduction of the Gross Income Based system in 2007, a system which gave a number of allowances only if (say) property were purchased in Gibraltar, or a Gibraltar pension established. This encouraged Gibraltarians to live in the jurisdiction, but the GSD government in 2007 perceived the state of affairs to be too one-sided and introduced a modified form of taxation called the 'Gross Income Based System' to counteract the effect of a low personal allowance under the traditional system (now called the Allowance Based System) and limited availability of allowances for cross border workers, the aim being to encourage compliance with tax legislation for cross border workers.

This is an example of a tax policy and legislation developed with the aim of taxing income generated in Gibraltar, whilst also ensuring fairness across different classes of individuals and harnessing the benefits that an open border territory has to offer. As a result, Gibraltar does not simply differentiate residents from non-residents, but considers a third type of individual; the person who works in and is present in Gibraltar every day, but who does not sleep overnight in the territory (i.e a cross border worker). The specific need for this three-way split is partly driven

82 Christophe Sohn, 'Modelling Cross-Border Integration: The Role of Borders as a Resource', [2014], *Geopolitics*

by the tax residence test contained in ITA 2010.

A three-tier system

The specific need for this three-way split between resident who sleeps in Gibraltar, resident who does not and non-resident is partly driven by the tax residence test contained in ITA 2010 which states that:

'ordinarily resident' when applied to an individual means an individual who irrespective of whether such individual is domiciled in Gibraltar or otherwise who in any year of assessment–

(a) is present in Gibraltar for a period of, or periods together amounting to, at least 183 days; or
(b) is present in Gibraltar in any year of assessment which is one of three consecutive years in which the total of the days on which the individual is present in Gibraltar exceeds 300,

and for the purposes of this definition presence in Gibraltar for any part of a 24 hour period commencing at midnight shall be counted as a day of presence whether or not any accommodation is used in Gibraltar'

Thus, the ITA ensures anyone who lives outside Gibraltar but is present in Gibraltar for 183 days is 'ordinarily resident', and the effect of the 'any presence is a day' rule is to make a cross border worker and a resident who has his home in Gibraltar indistinguishable.

It is the main thesis of this chapter that in order to behave responsibly in terms of the interests of Gibraltar and within the legal framework which is contained in the ITA 2010, the Government of Gibraltar has over successive administrations (though sometimes with different emphasis)[83] implemented a system which differentiates

83 For instance, see the exchanges between the now Chief Minister Fabian Picardo and the then Chief Minister Peter Caruana in the 2009 Budget Debate (Gibraltar Hansard, Report of the Proceedings of the Gibraltar Parliament 2009, p41), during which Mr Caruana and Mr Picardo debated the effect of the Gross Income Based system, and compare to the fact that Mr Picardo since in power has left the Gross Income Based system largely intact.

between those who sleep in Gibraltar, those who work in Gibraltar (both types of resident) and those who are non-resident, and it has done so by treating all fairly but through differing systems (the Gross Income Based system for example vs the Allowance Based System) which are variously applicable considering the differing personal and economic characteristics of those classes of tax payers.

Despite this complex legal and socio-economic backdrop, Gibraltar's tax policies and legislation must comply with international standards and work within the framework of local constitutional law. Whilst the European Convention on Human Rights has not been directly transposed into Gibraltar law, the UK extended its application to Gibraltar, so that the European Court of Human Rights could hear individual petitions from Gibraltar from January 2006. In addition, the Gibraltar Constitution Order 2006 contains many of the fundamental rights and freedoms which are contained in the European Convention on Human Rights. Gibraltar law therefore does expressly preserve a right of protection from discrimination, defined as 'affording different treatment to different persons attributable wholly or mainly to their respective descriptions by race, caste, place of or social origin, political or other opinions or affiliations, colour, language, sex, creed, property, birth or other states, or such other grounds as the European Court of Human Rights may, from time to time, determine to be discriminatory'.[84] However, an exception to this right arises in relation to 'any law so far as that law makes provision (...) for the appropriation of revenues or other funds of Gibraltar;'.[85] Arguably therefore, there is no prohibition against discrimination in the legislation relating to tax revenues.

To a certain extent, this is in line with the OECD Model, which should deliberately not be interpreted in an unduly broad manner, such that it could inadvertently also capture indirect discrimination.[86] It establishes a general

84 Gibraltar Constitution Order 2006, available online on: https://www.gibraltarlaws.gov.gi/uploads/constitution/Gibraltar_Constitution_Order_2006.pdf#viewer.action=download (Last accessed on 26th February 2024)

85 *Ibid*, s 14(4)(a)

86 OECD, 'Commentary on Article 24 Concerning Non-Discrimination' *Model Tax Convention on Income and on Capital: Condensed Version 2017* available online: https://read.oecd-ilibrary.org/taxation/model-tax-convention-on-income-and-on-capital-condensed-version-2017/commentary-on-article-24_mtc_cond-2017-27-en#page1> (Last accessed on 26th February 2024)

principle of equal treatment in the same or similar circumstances, save in the face of valid and objective justification. However, the treaty anti-discrimination clause is not intended to provide foreign nationals, non-residents, enterprises of other States or domestic enterprises owned or controlled by non-residents with a tax treatment that is more lenient or generous than that extended to nationals, residents or domestic enterprises owned or controlled by residents.[87] We feel that the increased costs and challenges associated with living in Gibraltar (and any other small jurisdiction) are sufficient, therefore, to ensure the three-tier tax regime in Gibraltar falls in line with international standards.

The meaning of the phrase 'tax resident'

Before considering the practical application of this distinction between the three tiers, it may be useful to carry out a detailed analysis of the meaning of the term 'resident' under Gibraltar tax legislation. An individual will be ordinarily resident in Gibraltar, whether or not they are domiciled in Gibraltar, if they are either

> '(a) present in Gibraltar for a period of, or periods together amounting to 183 days or
>
> (b) present in Gibraltar in any year of assessment which is one of three consecutive years in which the total of the days on which the individual is present in Gibraltar exceeds 300'.[88]

The definition of 'present' includes any part of a 24-hour period commencing at midnight, during which the individual is in Gibraltar, whether or not any accommodation is used in Gibraltar. The inclusion of any presence as signifying a whole day rather than a 'midnights' rule is not entirely unique (Spain for example uses a similar rule), however, it is clear that this particular choice has utility when considering a person who is a cross border worker (see Chapter 8) .

As a result, all cross-frontier workers who work in Gibraltar and sleep in Spain are considered ordinarily resident in Gibraltar for tax purposes. The equivalent definition of tax residence in Spain results in those workers also being considered resident in Spain for tax purposes, and thus dual resident.

---

87 *Ibid*

88 Income Tax Act 2010, s 74

The charge to tax on tax residents who sleep in Gibraltar

Ordinarily resident individuals are assessed on their worldwide income,[89] with the exception of any income specifically exempted by the legislation or income which is not specified under the charge to tax. The heads of charge to tax for individuals are income from property letting, employment income, benefits in kind, profits and gains from a business (self-employment), profession or vocation, pensions and annuities, dividends, income from a trust, funds income and any other income deemed to fall under any of those heads in accordance with the statutory anti-avoidance provisions.[90]

Individuals who are ordinarily resident only in Gibraltar, are not taxed on interest or investment income, or on capital. In addition, the definition of 'dividends' does not capture distributions from listed companies, which constitute investment income and are accordingly exempt from tax. It also excludes dividends issued by companies which do not themselves have income that is taxable in Gibraltar.

However, as previously mentioned, any income falling within the heads of charge is taxable in the hands of an ordinarily resident individual, regardless of source.[91] Except with respect to profits or gains from employment and self-employment income, these are only subject to tax in Gibraltar to the extent that all or part of the activities, administration, marketing or support functions of the trade, business, profession or vocation are performed in Gibraltar.

Tax resident cross-border workers from Spain

Given that daily presence in Gibraltar for work purposes will result in the cross-border worker meeting the test of 'ordinarily resident', these individuals are taxed in Gibraltar on the same basis as described above for those individuals who stay in Gibraltar overnight.

Accordingly, any gains or profits from any employment exercised in Gibraltar are taxable in Gibraltar, whether received by the cross-border worker in Gibraltar or not. This would include any benefits in kind by virtue of the exercise of that employment in Gibraltar.[92]

---

89 For further detail, see chapter 1

90 Income Tax Act 2010, Schedule 1 Table A, Table B and Table C

91 Income Tax Act 2010, s 11(2)

92 Income Tax Act 2010, s 17

In relation to self-employment income, the rule of indivisibility of trade is more likely to affect cross-border workers who work in Gibraltar but live in Spain. This rule dictates that a trade, business, profession or vocation is treated as indivisible and any activities of similar nature carried out in another jurisdiction by an ordinarily resident individual either in self-employment or as a member of a partnership including all receipts of employments undertaken in pursuance of the trade, business, profession or vocations, shall be regarded as part of the Gibraltar activities.[93] It is therefore not possible to argue that only a proportion of a business activity is carried out in Gibraltar and therefore liable to tax in Gibraltar.

This unity in the tax charge between those who both sleep in Gibraltar and those who do not, but who both work in Gibraltar means that the only method by which a differential between them can be established is through the allocation of allowances and benefits, or the availability of the dual income tax system.

Non-residents and those occasionally present in Gibraltar

If a person who is not ordinarily resident in Gibraltar should be present in Gibraltar for less than 30 days in aggregate within any year of assessment, they will not be liable to tax in Gibraltar on:

(a) emoluments from employment performed exclusively outside Gibraltar except for duties ancillary to that employment and performed in Gibraltar;
(b) fees in respect of the office of director of a company
(c) remuneration from any trade, profession, business or vocation where the trade, service, consultation or advice, or the activities ancillary to it, is performed, provided or given exclusively outside Gibraltar, other than in respect of any trade, business, profession, marketing or support functions of which are performed in Gibraltar.[94]

This essentially establishes a 30-day tax-free period for any non-resident person carrying out certain types of remunerated work on a purely temporary basis. However, it should be noted that whilst not taxable, such income must still be declared.

---

93 Income Tax Act 2010, Schedule 1 Table B, para 2(b)

94 Income Tax Act 2010, s19

Subject to this, non-residents are liable to tax in Gibraltar on any income accrued in or derived from Gibraltar, except on dividends.[95] In addition, if a non-resident person exercises any part of their employment in Gibraltar, they are liable to tax in Gibraltar on that proportion of their emoluments relating to the exercise of the employment in Gibraltar, irrespective of where or by whom the emoluments are paid.[96]

Different rates of tax apply to non-resident individuals; which on average result in a slightly higher level of tax paid. At the time of writing, the first £16,000 of taxable income for non-residents is taxed at 17%, with the remainder taxed at 39%. This is further discussed later in this chapter.

Double taxation relief

Any person who has paid or is liable to pay taxation in Gibraltar in respect of any profits or gains, regardless of where they were derived, and can demonstrate that they have paid or are liable to tax in another jurisdiction in respect of the same profit or gains, shall be entitled to relief from taxation paid or payable by them in respect of those profits or gains. This unilateral relief will be the lesser of:

(a) the taxation in Gibraltar in respect of the profits or gains; or
(b) the income tax in the jurisdiction in respect of that income.[97]

The relief available is reduced by any relief obtained in the other jurisdiction, and the amount of tax in the other jurisdiction is calculated without any reduction on account of any double taxation relief. Furthermore, the relief only applies to tax paid in a jurisdiction in, or from which, the revenue created by the underlying activity has been generated.[98]

95 Income Tax Act 2010, s 11(1), and Schedule 1 Table C, para (a)(ii)

96 See Chapter 2

97 Income Tax Act 2010, s 37

98 Income Tax Act 2010, s 37(8)

ABS and GIBS - Benefits for the resident individual

ABS and GIBS

Individuals have the choice of being taxed under two different systems.[99] One, known as the Allowances Based System, is the traditional system and, as its title suggests, provides for various allowances which can be deducted from an individual's income. This system is available to all ordinarily resident individuals, as well as to those non-residents who are in receipt of a pension accruing in Gibraltar. Most allowances are subject to a reduction of 1/12 for each complete calendar month within which the individual is not ordinarily resident in Gibraltar during the year of assessment. For more information on the allowances and deductions, please refer to the table below.

The other system is known as the Gross Income Based System, under which tax rates are lower, but the taxpayer is entitled to fewer deductions. This system was introduced to 'reduce the tax burden of those who by their personal circumstances cannot benefit from the traditional system, which is very high rates and very high allowances.'[100]

Allowances/Deductions

The various allowances and deductions are detailed in Gibraltar legislation. Most of these are only applicable to those who have elected to be assessed on the Allowance Based System. However, there are a number of deductions for similar items which are also available to those on the Gross Income Based System, albeit subject to different requirements and/or amounts. For those individuals who qualify for a number of allowances and deductions, the Allowance Based System is likely to be the most favourable. Those who do not qualify for a sufficient quantity of allowances and deductions will benefit from the lower effective tax rate under the Gross Income Based System. In this respect, individuals are asked to provide sufficient information on their tax returns, so that the Income Tax Office can

---

99 Rates of Tax Rules 1989

100 Hansard 2009 Report of the proceedings of the Gibraltar Parliament, The Sixth Meeting of the Eleventh Parliament, 17th March 2009

conduct an assessment to determine which system is the most favourable.

As can be seen from the table below, the allowances and deductions are largely for the benefit of individuals who are ordinarily resident in Gibraltar. For those who become, or cease to be, ordinarily resident part-way through a given tax year, most allowances and deductions are reduced by 1/12 for each complete calendar month within which the individual is no longer ordinarily resident in Gibraltar.

Main Allowances / Deductions	Description	Residents who sleep in Gibraltar	Cross-border workers	Non Resident
ALLOWANCE BASED SYSTEM [101][1]				
* Personal	Amount deducted from assessable income. Allowance is reduced by 1/12 for each calendar month the individual is not resident in Gibraltar.	✓	✓	✗
*Spouse & Civil Partner	Amount deducted from assessable income. Available to an ordinarily resident (a) living with Spouse or civil partner or (b) paying alimony / maintenance in respect of a dissolved or annulled marriage or civil partnership or (c) making payments in accordance with a court order or a separation agreement to a spouse or civil partner from which separated. Allowance is reduced by 1/12 for each calendar month the individual is not resident Gibraltar.	✓	✓	✗

101 [1] Income Tax (Allowances, Deductions and Exemptions) Rules 1992

*Age	Amount deducted from assessable income. Available to an ordinarily resident man who is 65 years old or more or an ordinarily resident woman who is 60 years old or more. Allowance is reduced by 1/12 for each calendar month the individual is not resident.	✓	✓	×
*Low Earnings	If earning less than the applicable amount, then no tax payable.	✓	✓	×
*Nursery School	Amount deducted from assessable income. Available to an ordinarily resident with a child who attends private nursery in Gibraltar for a full school year. Although this deduction is available to cross-border workers it is seldom claimed given that cross-border workers normally enrol their children in nurseries in Spain.	✓	✓	×
*Child	Amount deducted from assessable income. Available for ordinarily resident's first child only and must be under 16 years old and in full time education. Allowance is reduced by 1/12 for each calendar month the individual is not resident.	✓	✓	×

*Child Educated Abroad	Amount deducted from assessable income. Available for ordinarily resident's child who is 16 years old or over and is in full time education outside of Gibraltar. The individual claiming this deduction must reside in Gibraltar and the child must be studying abroad via the Department of Education. The individual must not be entitled to a similar allowance or deduction in any other country in respect of the child.	✓	✗	✗
*Parent of Disabled Individual	Amount deducted from assessable income. Available to an ordinarily resident who is the parent of an unmarried individual who resides with him/her and suffers from a specific bodily or mental disability. Prohibited from claiming this allowance if already claim either of the 2 allowances listed immediately above.	✓	✓	✗
*Blind	Amount deducted from assessable income. Available to an ordinarily resident who proves by production of a certificate that he or his spouse or civil partner has effectively lost his or her sight. Allowance is reduced by 1/12 for each calendar month the individual is not resident.	✓	✓	✗
*Maintenance of child	Amount deducted from assessable income. Available to an ordinarily resident who has custody of an unmarried child and is not entitled to spouse allowance. Allowance is reduced by 1/12 for each calendar month the individual is not resident.	✓	✓	✗

***Dependant Relative**	Amount deducted from assessable income. Available to an ordinarily resident who maintains (a) a relative who is incapacitated by old age or infirmity or (b) his or her widowed mother (whether incapacitated or not) and being a person whose total income does not exceed the maximum threshold. The deduction is higher if the dependent is ordinarily resident in Gibraltar. Allowance reduced by 1/12 for each calendar month the individual is not resident.	✓	✓	✗
***Medical Insurance**	Amount deducted from assessable income. Available to an ordinarily resident who pays medical insurance for himself/herself, his/her spouse or civil partner or his/her dependent children. The insurance policy must have been approved by the Commissioner of Tax. Allowance is reduced by 1/12 for each calendar month the individual is not resident.	✓	✓	✗
***Apprentice**	Amount deducted from assessable income. Available to an ordinarily resident who proves that he was an apprentice. Allowance is reduced by 1/12 for each calendar month the individual is not resident.	✓	✓	✗

House	There are two types of Home Purchase Allowance: 1. Available to an ordinarily resident in respect of his/her main residence. Allowance can be claimed in full in a single tax year, or split over various years. Allowance split between spouses / civil partners living in same residence. Available to an ordinarily resident who purchases a property for his/her child[102][2]. 2. Available to an ordinarily resident, capped amount each year. Can only claim this allowance once[103][3].	✓	✗	✗
Mortgage Interest	Amount deducted from assessable income. Available to an ordinarily resident in respect of a property he or she occupies. Capped loan amount. Also available for parking space subject to restrictions.	✓	✗	✗
GROSS INCOME BASED SYSTEM [104][4]				
Main Residential Property[105][5]	Amount deducted from assessable income. Available to an ordinarily resident in respect of his/her first main residence. Restricted to half of allowance amount in any tax year. Allowance split between spouses / civil partners living in same residence.	✓	✗	✗

102 [2] Home Purchase (Deductions) Rules 1989

103 [3] Home Purchase (Special Deduction) Rules 2004

104 [4] Income Tax (Allowances, Deductions and Exemptions) Rules 1992

105 [5] Home Purchase (Deductions) Rules 1989

Approved Pension	Amount deducted from assessable income. Available to an individual who contributes to an approved pension scheme. The pension scheme must have been approved by the Commissioner of Income Tax. In practice, only Gibraltar based pension schemes receive approval.	✓	✓	✓
***Medical Insurance**	Amount deducted from assessable income. Available to an ordinarily resident who pays medical insurance for himself/herself, his/her spouse or civil partner or his/her dependent children. The insurance policy must have been approved by the Commissioner of Tax. Allowance is reduced by 1/12 for each calendar month the individual is not resident.	✓	✓	✗
Renewable Energy[106][6]	Amount deducted from assessable income. Available for the installation of solar thermal systems or PV panels to supply electricity to households. Allowance is applied over two years and is applicable per household.	✓	✓	✓
Mortgage Interest	Amount deducted from assessable income. Available to an ordinarily resident in respect of a property he or she occupies. Capped loan amount. Also available for parking space subject to restrictions.	✓	✗	✗

106 [6] Energy Performance (Deductions) Rules 2018

Property Frontage Enhancement[107][7]	Amount deducted from assessable income. Available to any person who has an interest in a building within a tax-deductible property zone and who has incurred approved expenditure on repair or enhancement of the frontage and/or roof of the building	✓	✗	✓

*** These allowances / deductions are also available to non-resident individuals who are in receipt of a pension accruing in Gibraltar.**

A different tax rate for non-resident individuals (Rates of Tax Rules 1989 Rule 3)

Gibraltar applies different rates of tax to resident and non-resident individuals. The legislation differentiates between the following types of tax payer:

Residents with assessable income on the Allowances Based System and non-residents in receipt of a pension accruing in Gibraltar

The allowance based system rates of tax will generally apply to residents who are assessed under the Allowance Based System and non-residents who receive pensions which accrue in Gibraltar. These tax payers are able to claim more allowances and deductions than the other types of tax payer (please see table above for more information on allowances and deductions).

Residents and non-residents with assessable income on Gross Income Based System

Both residents and non-residents can elect to be subject to the Gross Income Based System; the rates of tax will depend on whether they earn over the applicable threshold in the relevant year of assessment. The rates are lower than under the allowance based system.

107 [7] Income Tax (Deduction Of Approved Expenditure On Premises In Tax Deductible Property Zone) Rules 2010

Depending on an individual's circumstances, it may be more favourable for an individual to be on the Gross Income Based System rather than the Allowance Based System (or vice versa). The Income Tax Office automatically calculates each individual's assessable income under the Allowance Based System and the Gross Income Based System, and will allocate the individual to the most favourable system.

Other Non-residents not under an alternative regime

This category of tax payer includes non-residents who do not elect to be assessed under the Gross Income Based System and do not receive a pension accruing in Gibraltar. There is a special rate set by Rule 3(1) of the Rates of Tax Rules (1989).

Non-residents who qualify under alternative regimes

There are alternative taxation systems for individuals who meet certain criteria. The most popular of these schemes are the category 2 status and the High Executives Possessing Specialist Skills status.

High Net Worth Individuals

Category 2 (Cat 2) Status

The Cat 2 status is an attractive scheme for non-resident individuals who are looking to become Gibraltar taxpayers. The purpose of this status, from Gibraltar's perspective, is to attract high net worth individuals to Gibraltar.

In order to apply for Cat 2 status, an individual must meet certain criteria, the main ones being the exclusive use of residential accommodation of a particular approved category and not having been a resident in Gibraltar for the prescribed period prior to the date of the application.[108] Although there is no requirement for the individual to make a specific investment in Gibraltar (other than purchasing or renting approved residential accommodation), a number of Cat 2 individuals end up solidifying their ties to Gibraltar by investing in the local community.

The main advantage of obtaining the Cat 2 certificate is that the person will only be assessable to tax on a capped amount of his/her income. This cap does not apply to income accrued in or derived from Gibraltar. Cat 2 individuals are taxed

108 Qualifying (Category 2) Individuals Rules 2004

under the Allowances Based System at the highest rate, and are not entitled to claim any deductions.

A Cat 2 individual must have approved accommodation available for their exclusive use all year around, although the legislation is silent on minimum days required Cat 2 status does not offer citizenship or shield any individual from becoming tax resident in a different country.

Cat 2 status can be differentiated from the Non-Domiciled status in the UK in many respects, including those listed below (a non-exhaustive list):

- there are no requirements with respect to a Cat 2 individual being domiciled in another jurisdiction. The individual can intend to be permanently based in Gibraltar, or conversely, they may wish to spend minimal time in Gibraltar. The only requirement, with respect to ties to Gibraltar, is that the individual must not have been a resident in Gibraltar for the prescribed period prior to the date of the Cat 2 application.
- Cat 2 individuals pay tax in Gibraltar (subject to a cap) irrespective whether they have any assessable income.

Cat 2 status can also be differentiated from residency by investment schemes considered by the OECD to be 'high risk'. According to the OECD, 'CBI/RBI [Citizenship by Investment / Residency by Investment] schemes can be misused to undermine the Common Reporting Standard due diligence procedures. This may lead to inaccurate or incomplete reporting under the CRS, in particular when not all jurisdictions of tax residence are disclosed to the Financial Institution. Such a scenario could arise where an individual does not actually or not only reside in the CBI/RBI jurisdiction, but claims to be resident for tax purposes only in such jurisdiction and provides his Financial Institution with supporting documentation issued under the CBI/RBI scheme, for example a certificate of residence, ID card or passport.'[109] This OECD guidance specifies that these schemes can undermine CRS due diligence procedures by allowing individuals to claim to be resident for tax purposes; this is not possible for an individual with Cat 2 status, as this status does not grant tax residency in Gibraltar. It is also important to note that

109 Please see further: https://www.oecd.org/tax/automatic-exchange/crs-implementation-and-assistance/residence-citizenship-by-investment/ (Last accessed on 26th February 2024)

Gibraltar has worked hard to conclude 27 Tax Information Exchange Agreements which require Gibraltar to exchange information to the OECD standard with 27 countries around the world[110]. This is of course aside from the fact that the Multilateral Convention on Mutual Administrative Assistance in Tax Matters was extended to Gibraltar which has obviated the need for further bilateral Tax Information Exchange Agreements.[111]

High Executives Possessing Specialist Skills (HEPSS)

The employment of High Executives Possessing Specialist Skills (HEPSS) in Gibraltar is governed by a comprehensive legal framework designed to attract and retain highly skilled professionals. Gibraltar, known for its thriving financial and business sectors, recognises the significant impact that HEPSS individuals can have on its economic development. As such, specific laws and regulations have been established to facilitate the recruitment, employment and residency of HEPSS professionals in the jurisdiction.

HEPSS status is a tax status that can be obtained by employers in Gibraltar on behalf of employees who meet certain criteria. The individual must occupy a high executive or senior management position, possess specialist skills and earn more than the threshold. Furthermore, the employee must prove that those skills are not readily available in Gibraltar and that they are important for the economic development and growth of Gibraltar. The individual must also have exclusive use of residential accommodation of a particular approved category and not have been resident in Gibraltar for the prescribed period prior to the date of the application.[112]

Similar to the Cat 2 status, the main advantage of obtaining the HEPSS status is that the person will only be assessable to tax on a capped amount of his/her income. HEPSS individuals are taxed under the Gross Income Based System.

---

110 https://www.gibraltarfinance.gi/about-us/international-cooperation (Last accessed on 26th February 2024)

111 Please see further: https://www.gibraltar.gov.gi/uploads/Income%20Tax%20Office/docs/(TAX)_GI%20EOIR%20RELATIONSHIPS%20MATRIX.pdf (Last accessed on 26th February 2024)

112 High Executive Possessing Specialist Skills Rules 2008

Conclusion

Gibraltar is unique. That much is acknowledged by all those who have either lived on it, worked on it or have known it. It must protect itself and it must attract new talent and workers from across the border. This confluence of unique inputs has moulded Gibraltar's taxation system to service the needs of the three different groups we have talked about in this chapter. With almost 50% of its workforce being cross border workers in 2003[113] who contribute to the economy but also export their wages, it has an economic imperative to implement an unusual system. The authors believe that it has done this through the targeted granting of allowances to encourage Gibraltar-based activity which gives rise to a wider benefit to Gibraltar. In parallel to this, it also implements a simple and generous tax regime in the Gross Income Based System for those who live in the Campo area. Finally it offers attractive regimes available only to those who are non-residents to encourage them to bring their talent to Gibraltar. We believe that this three-tier system has contributed to the success and development of Gibraltar over the last twenty years; that it may well be modified in the future,[114] but that it will continue to exhibit this three-tier characteristic.

113 Supra 66

114 At the time of writing, there is a proposal for a consultation on the simplification of the personal taxation system which may well merge the two GIB and ABS systems, though we believe that preserving the distinction between those who sleep in Gibraltar and those who work here will be unavoidable.

Chapter 3

FORM GIVES NO BENEFIT

The Principle of Tax Neutrality in Administrative Matters

Ivan Gomez, Caroline Lane and Grahame Jackson

Abstract

The aim of a tax neutral system is that any decisions made by the taxpayer should be made on their economic strengths rather than on any potential tax incentive or disincentive. This chapter explores the theory behind tax neutrality and its benefits, the key features of a neutral tax system and its challenges in implementing them. The chapter discusses how the concept of tax neutrality applies to Gibraltar's tax system and whether its tax system is effective in achieving neutrality.

Introduction

The traditional focus for the discussion of tax neutrality has been the effect on international capital/investment inflows and outflow. That is as 'Export Neutrality' and 'Import Neutrality'. These two concepts are important in the context of international taxation but they are not all that there is when it comes to tax neutrality. Neutrality in its widest sense can be defined thus:

> The basic concept is simple: generally the tax system should strive to be neutral so that decisions are made on their economic merits and not for tax reasons.[115]

---

115 Jason Furman Testimony Before the U.S. Senate Committee on Finance Hearing on 'Tax: Fundamentals in Advance of Reform,' April 15, 2008

In a neutral system, a taxpayer's reaction to a specific tax or tax related provision would be the same as if such tax or such provisions did not exist. [116] This is what a tax neutral system should attempt to achieve. This is as true globally at the point of an investor choosing a jurisdiction, as it is internally in every jurisdiction at the point of an investor choosing the form of an investment in which to invest. Every tax related provision can have an effect on behaviour if it can increase or decrease the tax burden dependent on which choice the taxpayer makes. The aim of neutrality is to eliminate this effect.

A tax neutral system should not favour any form of investment, economic activity or consumption pattern. As a result, in a tax neutral system the rationale for the behaviour of a taxpayer should never be influenced by tax considerations. Globally, if a tax neutral approach is taken, capital would be invested wherever the return would be highest and not where one form of investment or jurisdiction would enable the investor to achieve more beneficial taxation rates. [117] A tax neutral system therefore should be effective in promoting economic growth, certainty and fairness, and attempt to minimise economic distortions by promoting decisions based on economic fundamentals. A tax neutral system is efficient.

A tax system which is not founded on the principle of tax neutrality would enable artificially created economies targeting tax-adapted behaviours to flourish to the detriment of jurisdictions, or forms of investment and industries which might otherwise be favoured by the investor were it not for tax considerations. This is called tax bias. Tax bias can be positive, where the tax system favours certain industries or forms of investment by providing them with preferential tax rates or rules or negative, where the tax system penalises certain industries or forms of investment. Positive tax biases include incentives such as tax deductions or tax credits and negative tax bias includes mostly higher tax rates. We can imagine a world in which a country wishes to encourage economic activity in an economically depressed region by lowering their corporation tax. This would be a non-neutral system.

This is not to say that tax neutrality is ever completely achievable. It is clear that some forms of taxation provisions are deliberately designed not to be neutral. For example, mortgage interest relief (see Chapter 2) is designed to reward those who purchase property, or an allowance related to raising children is designed to ease

116 Kristina Ståhl, Aktiebeskattning och fria kapitalrörelser, Iustus förlag, 1996, p. 89.

117 Ruth Mason, 'Tax Discrimination and Capital Neutrality' (2010) 2010 World Tax J 126

the burden of having children, tobacco taxes have gone beyond a revenue raising provision and now amount to a deterrence on certain behaviour. It is the nature of taxes, politics and how they interact in the modern world that pure neutrality cannot be practically achieved.

Importance of Tax Neutrality

Whilst the aim of tax neutrality is to ensure that decisions are not made on the basis of tax implications, its effect is to ensure an equitable distribution of capital investment based on economic reality. In addition, the object of achieving tax neutrality is crucial in order to maintain a fair and just tax system as it treats all economic activities and individuals equally, without causing one to be more advantageous than the other, whilst simultaneously reducing misallocation of resources and artificial market inefficiencies. In other words, a tax neutral system has not only an economic outcome but also a moral strength which comes from treating all taxpayers equally.

In a tax neutral jurisdiction, individuals and businesses would base their decisions on genuine economic considerations rather than tax implications. This encourages productive activities, investment, and innovation which fosters economic growth and stability. This also prevents behaviour which is driven on the basis of tax thereby undermining societal goals, such as artificially inflating expenses or shifting profits to lower-tax jurisdictions.

A fair tax system hinges on treating all taxpayers equally and transparently with the burden of funding public services in a tax neutral system distributed impartially among individuals and businesses. By avoiding preferential treatment or disincentives, neutrality upholds the principle of horizontal equity where individuals in similar situations are taxed similarly. The certainty that comes with a tax neutral system should also promote compliance amongst taxpayers.

By avoiding targeted tax incentives or penalties, tax neutrality minimizes market distortions. For instance, subsidies to certain industries can artificially inflate their growth, leading to misallocation of resources. Conversely, punitive taxes on particular goods or services may create black markets or discourage legitimate economic activities. The Selective Employment Tax introduced in the United Kingdom in 1966, where every employer would be levied a tax of 25 shillings per male employee and 12 shillings and 6 pence per female employee, is a clear illustration of punitive taxes aimed to artificially encourage investment in the manufacturing industry by way of tax incentives and the 'punishment' of those industries deemed to be unwanted. The Selective Employment Taxes paid by employers were later refunded to employers in the manufacturing industry together with an additional premium per employee. This scheme was intended to provide an incentive to the manufacturing industry at the expense of the services industry. The rationale behind this was to encourage investment in industries that promoted and contributed to UK exports in a changing world market. The UK was in the process of deindustrialising and the Selective Employment Tax was short lived, being repealed in 1973.

Tax neutrality reduces these artificial instabilities by creating a more stable and predictable economic environment. When explaining the purpose and concept of tax neutrality in testimony to the U.S. Senate Committee on Finance, Jason Furman, former director of the National Economic Council of the United States, provided a key example:

> 'in an efficient economic system people would choose between chocolate chip cookies and oatmeal cookies based on their own personal tastes and the costs of these products. If policymakers imposed a tax on chocolate chip cookies but not on oatmeal cookies the result would be that people would now factor taxes into their choice about which type of cookie to consume—and possibly end up consuming the less desirable cookie because it was cheaper.'[118]

A non-neutral tax system would therefore also lead individuals and businesses to dedicate great effort towards changing the form of their activities to reduce their overall tax liabilities, instead of dedicating such time and resources to the business itself.

One example of the effects of a non-neutral system is that investment decisions made by large multi-nationals are influenced by the tax regimes of the various jurisdictions in question[119]. This can be the case not only in the establishment of

118 Jason Furman Testimony Before the U.S. Senate Committee on Finance Hearing on "Tax: Fundamentals in Advance of Reform," April 15, 2008

119 Much of this effect, at least for the largest tax payers will be neutralized by the introduction of what is known as "Pillar 2" in the years following 2024. Pillar 2 amounts to a global minimum tax rate of 15% taxed on a globally harmonized tax base. It

subsidiaries in low tax jurisdictions but also the location of factories and large installations. This effect results in loss of revenue for jurisdictions where either the economic activity occurs but tax is being paid elsewhere or there is relocation of that economic activity to another jurisdiction in the search for a lower tax burden. This has resulted in the international community seeking to narrow the gap between the jurisdiction where the economic activity occurs and the taxpayer's resident jurisdiction, with initiatives such as the economic substance rules, of which the European Union is supportive, and which historically tax-competitive jurisdictions are now adopting.[120]

The distortion of business decisions can also be seen when jurisdictions offer tax incentives to certain industries which lead to overinvestment in that sector, causing inefficiencies and potentially leaving other sectors underdeveloped. A lack of tax neutrality could also have consequences on sectors such as innovation, where research and development tax credits may encourage innovation, but also prompt companies to engage in artificial research and development primarily for tax benefits where there may be no need for this, potentially diverting resources from more productive activities.

That is not to say that governments do not and should not deliberately deviate from tax neutrality in order to encourage certain behaviours. They often do, and historically it has been a method by which economic activity has been directed by the authorities. In practice the principle of tax neutrality is never entirely achieved, to do so would be to surrender a major tool which governments have in their economic policy toolkit[121]. In fact, Gibraltar has a number of tax credits, incentives and relief in both its corporate and its individual tax systems to encourage taxpayers to act in a manner which the authorities deem to be of benefit to the jurisdiction. However, what can be achieved is a removal of all those unintended or legacy provisions which impact on tax neutrality without policy intent or which give rise

---

results from the OECD work on BEPS and the Inclusive Framework.

120 See, for example, Council of the European Union: The EU list of non-cooperative jurisdictions for tax purposes - Bermuda: final legislation and assessment under criterion 2. FISC 276 23 May 2019.

121 Hong Kong's system in the post war pre-return to China was probably one of the most successful attempts to achieve tax neutrality. For an in-depth discussion see, Littlewood, Michael, 'Taxation without representation – the history of Hong Kong's troublingly successful tax system', Hong Kong University Press, 2010

to unintended outcomes.

In the case of individuals, high property taxes, for example, may encourage relocation to another jurisdiction based solely on tax considerations. This clearly leads to an unequal distribution of economic activity. High marginal tax rates on income may also discourage individuals from working longer hours or from seeking higher-paying jobs, and encourage capital disposals (which in Gibraltar are not taxed) rather than long term investment in income generating businesses. This is likely to lead to a reduced recruitment pool and could contribute to a lower overall economic productivity. Tax policies that favour immediate consumption over savings, such as low consumption taxes and low savings-related deductions, or high tax on "unearned income", can discourage households from saving for the future. This can lead to insufficient retirement funds and increased dependence on social welfare programs.

These examples demonstrate how tax considerations can distort economic decisions, both in global business and in individuals, leading to long-term inefficiencies, unequal outcomes, and unintended negative impacts overall economic performance. Tax neutrality aims to mitigate these distortions and promote more rational economic choices.

Three types of neutrality

When considering the impact of taxation on investment, the effect of taxation should neither discourage taxpayers from conducting capital import (i.e. inbound investment) (this is called 'capital import neutrality', 'CIN') nor should it discourage taxpayers from conducting capital export (i.e. outbound investment) (this is called 'capital export neutrality', 'CEN'), nor should it encourage decisions as to legal form to be taken based on tax treatment (this is what we will call 'administrative neutrality'). Again, the benchmark to assess whether a taxation system is neutral is to make a comparison with the situation if no tax had been levied.[122] That is, would the same outcome have occurred if no tax had been levied.

122 Richard Abel Musgrave, 'Criteria for Foreign Tax Credit', in Baker (ed). Taxation and Operations Abroad. (Princeton: Tax Institute, 1960), pp. 83–93. Later Peggy Musgrave also further writes about the distinction of CEN and CIN. See Musgrave, P. B. 'Taxation of Foreign Investment Income, An Economic Analysis'. Johns Hopkins Press,

The concepts of capital export neutrality, capital income neutrality and administrative neutrality are key elements in what makes up a tax system.[123] They should be key elements in any successful neutral tax system for the reasons set out below. With CIN and CEN the provisions required to achieve both capital export neutrality and capital import neutrality are not necessarily the same and on occasion can be at odds with each other.

Capital Export Neutrality

Under a system which properly achieves CEN, investors would not be taxed differently whether they invest in their home jurisdiction or abroad, thereby, ensuring an efficient allocation of global capital influenced only by economic/ commercial decisions.[124] In order for a tax system to satisfy CEN, the capital should be invested in the same location where such capital would have been invested had there been no taxes. The only method by which this can be ensured (that is, which gives a guaranteed CEN result rather than a practical outcome) is to tax entities in their jurisdiction of residence alone (no source based element), this would mean all income wherever generated is taxed according to the system of the home jurisdiction, and as long as that system did not differentiate between domestic and foreign income then CEN would be achieved.[125]

Capital Import Neutrality

The other side of this coin is the taxing carried out by the jurisdiction into which investment is to be made. For a capital importing jurisdiction it has two objectives:

1963, p.1–140, reprinted in Musgrave, P. R. Tax Policy in the Global Economy: Selected Essays of Peggy R.Musgrave, Cheltenham: Edward Elgar, 2002, p. 1–470

123 Peggy B. Richman, *Taxation of Foreign Investment Income: An Economic Analysis* (1963); Peggy B. Musgrave, *United States Taxation of Foreign Investment Income* (1969).

124 Gary Clyde Hufbauer and Ariel Assa, 'US Taxation of Foreign Income' (2007), Peterson Institute for International Economics

125 Fadi Shaheen, 'International Tax Neutrality: Reconsiderations' (2007), 27 Va Tax Review 203

the first is that inward investment should not be discouraged by bars to entry such as differentials in treatment between inward investors and domestic investors. Conversely a jurisdiction should not handicap its domestic investors and thus discourage home grown economic development. The solution to these two competing imperatives is equal treatment. In order to achieve CIN a jurisdiction should tax a resident and foreign investor in the same way regardless of where the foreign investor resides and the tax rates which are applicable to the foreign investor. Under CIN, the jurisdiction in which the activity is taking place should assess domestic and foreign investors in the same way. On the other hand, foreign investments made by residents should be exempted by the home jurisdiction in order to ensure that such capital is subject only to tax in the jurisdiction in which such income is earned.

Although the intention behind CIN is to achieve competitive neutrality, this may be distorted if the foreign investor's home jurisdiction does not implement the same approach. The issue therefore arises, that CIN cannot be achieved by jurisdictions on a unilateral basis as it must be implemented globally in order to work in the most efficient way.

Administrative Neutrality

The third form of neutrality and one which is much more within the remit of the Government of Gibraltar (which is, of course, a devolved administration given Gibraltar's position as an overseas territory) is that of what we will call 'Administrative Neutrality'. The aim of 'Administrative Neutrality' is to ensure that form and substance are aligned. In other words, that an investor should have no preference to a particular form (that is entity, or legal arrangement) or other behaviour with tax effect based on the taxation treatment of one form or choice over another.

As an example of the way that form can impact tax treatment in a non-neutral way, let us imagine a jurisdiction in which self-employed trade income is taxed at 50%, but corporation tax is set at 15%. In addition to this, there is no tax on dividend income. In this scenario the taxation system would encourage the creation of limited companies, because a self-employed person would pay an effective rate of 50% on his trade profits, but if he incorporated a company, the company would pay 15% on its profits and he would receive his dividends tax free, giving an effective rate of 15%.

This is, of course a highly simplified example of a non-neutral taxation provision which would defeat administrative neutrality. However, in a complex economy with multiple different legal forms interacting with different incentives, then more complex examples will arise if the tax authorities are not vigilant as to these possible outcomes. A real life example can be seen in the use of Scottish limited partnerships in tax planning. Scottish limited partnerships have legal personality but are also treated as transparent for the purposes of the United Kingdom taxation system (a combination of characteristics not exhibited by English partnerships). Scottish limited partnerships have become popular in planning to such an extent that between 2011 and 2016, the number of Scottish limited partnerships increased by 237% as opposed to 42% for their English equivalents.[126]

As discussed above, an economy in which decisions are made for reasons other than of economic substance is an inefficient one. In our example, given the tax gain to be had by having a limited company, one would expect an industry to grow up around providing such services, an industry which is not adding value to the economy but merely diverting artificial tax gains. In addition, those for whom limited companies are not suitable would find themselves trapped in a structure they do not need. In other words, a decision skewed by tax considerations would have an increased likelihood of being an unsuitable decision.

Import and Export Neutrality in Gibraltar

The Gibraltarian taxation system does not deliver neutrality in relation to capital import and export. This statement is simply true and that truth is why this chapter is titled 'Form Gives No Benefit' and not 'Neutrality above All!', or something similar. This can be seen throughout the taxation system. For example:

(i) Certain non-residents pay a higher tax rate under the provisions of Rule 3(1) of the Rates of Tax Rules 1989 thus treating imported capital differently from that of domestically generated capital. This rule obviously encourages the establishment of the investor in Gibraltar whether by

126 SNP reiterates calls for action on Scottish limited partnerships in manifesto | Accountancy Daily

physically relocating here or establishing a company which is resident here.

(ii) Non-residents are exempted from taxation on dividends paid by companies which have accrued and derived their income in Gibraltar.[127] Whereas a Gibraltar resident would pay tax on such a dividend. This encourages capital importation, but in order to take advantage of this exemption foreign residnets would have to establish some form of local presence.

(iii) The territorial base of the corporate taxation system means that income generated by sources outside Gibraltar is not subject to tax whereas that generated by sources within Gibraltar is, thus encouraging capital exportation.[128]

There are many possible justifications for this system, both in principle and as historic explanations for its development. Gibraltar has always been a trading post which had as one of its goals the encouragement of trade at an important crossroads. The encouragement of capital exportation is entirely consistent with that. Whilst, as with any small close-knit community, Gibraltar is vulnerable to, or at least wary of, having its social and economic cohesion disrupted by large inflows of capital devoid of any physical connection or psychological investment in the place itself. There is a large investment of time and effort in being resident in Gibraltar, as anyone who lives here will confirm, and it would be entirely consistent for many people to believe that those who do not take the uncertainty of life in a jurisdiction as small as Gibraltar should not benefit on an equal footing to those who do. These matters impact on policy makers, and as a result CIN and CEN are unachievable in today's Gibraltar.

Consistent treatment across legal forms – Administrative Neutrality

These policy and political considerations are absent when considering Administrative Neutrality. The 'good' of Administrative Neutrality is underpinned

127 Income Tax Act 2010, Schedule 1 Table C Class 1

128 Income Tax Act 2010 s11(1)

by a more basic position; a tax system which does not take into account the fact that taxpayers may choose legal forms specifically for their tax treatment and which does not seek to equalise the tax treatment across legal forms will not achieve an efficient economy, merely encourage wasteful and inefficient behaviours.

A taxation system which hopes to achieve what can loosely be described as 'administrative neutrality' cannot tolerate such outcomes. If avoidance is the use of procedures and arrangements devoid of economic reality to create a tax benefit at odds to the legislative intent of the legislature, then a system which equalises treatment of forms and outcomes based on legal but not commercial differences will discourage or eliminate avoidance. It is in the gaps which non-neutral administrative provisions create where tax avoidance flourishes and why an administratively neutral system is important so as not to afford taxpayers with opportunities for avoidance.

In the above sections we have discussed what it is to achieve neutrality in the systems of taxation in principle. The aim of this work, however, is not to be a general discourse on international taxation, but one which deals with the taxation system of Gibraltar, and so we must turn our attention to the practical outcomes of the Gibraltar system.

Gibraltar's system can be described as 'administratively neutral' because the form of investment does not provide the taxpayer with a benefit from the tax liability of a particular investment, hence 'form gives no benefit'.

There are numerous forms in which a taxpayer may elect to invest. The below examples assumes that the investment in question generates Gibraltar taxable income. A taxpayer may invest:

- in their own name;
- as a shareholder in a company;
- by settling a trust;
- through a fund;
- as a partner in a general partnership;
- as a limited partner through a limited liability partnership.

A taxpayer may elect to invest through any of the above vehicles or any combination of the above vehicles. The tax liability in Gibraltar will ultimately be exactly the same. The only element which may differ would be a deferment of the tax liability depending on the vehicle used i.e. the point in time at which the tax liability is due. We give a number of worked examples below; all are based on the assumption that any trade income is accrued in and derived from Gibraltar:

(i) **Personal trade activity**
David carries out a trade as a self-employed person and will pay a maximum effective rate of 27%[129] on his trade profits.

(ii) **Trade Activity in Partnership**
David goes into partnership with his brother Andrew. They are taxed as if self-employed, at a maximum effective rate of 27% on their trade profits.

(iii) **Trading through a company**
David and Andrew establish a company (D and Co) to carry out the trade of their partnership. They pay themselves a wage, on which they pay a maximum 27% effective rate. After this wage has been taken into account, the company will pay 12.5% on its trade profits. When the company dividends its profits out, they will pay 27% maximum effective rate on the dividend but will receive a 12.5% credit for the tax paid by the company (thus eliminating double taxation). The effective combined rate paid by them and the company together is a maximum of 27%, identical to what they would have paid if they had earned the money direct, and identical to the tax payable on their wage.

(iv) **They establish a trust**
David and Andrew want to carry out some succession planning. They establish a trust to hold their shares in D and Co. Just as before, the company pays 12.5% in tax. It then distributes its profits to the Trustee who hold the shares on trust. The trustee has a tax rate of 12.5% which is eliminated by a tax credit granted by the company. When the trust makes a distribution, the income distributed is matched to the distribution and the credit rolls over to the beneficiary who will pay the difference between the 12.5 % paid by the company and the maximum 27% effective rate. Over the whole process, no more than 27% effective taxation is to be paid.

129 This is the maximum effective rate as at the time of writing in December 2023.

This pattern is repeated throughout the system:[130] whether there is a fund, or a Limited Liability Partnership, the ultimate outcome is the same, or should approximate to the same. The interaction of credits and exemptions means that a given piece of taxable income which finds its way to an individual resident in Gibraltar will never be subject to a burden of more than 27% effective rate.

The form selected by a taxpayer for their investment and which dictates how that investment is taxed in Gibraltar seems therefore to give no tax benefit. The tax system is designed in a way to attempt only to establish where the income-generating activity has taken place and to tax such income accordingly. The conclusion from this is that investors in Gibraltar will elect the form of investment that makes more sense to them from an economic or practical perspective, but never from a tax perspective. On the basis of the above discussion, it can therefore be concluded that Gibraltar has been successful, in general at least, in implementing this element of tax neutrality into its tax system.

Conclusion

Gibraltar's tax system deviates far from tax neutrality in terms of import and export neutrality, that is undeniable. However, as discussed, there are political and policy reasons for that effect. In terms of administrative neutrality, the design of the system is such that on a high level, form does give no benefit. Modifications to the tax law of Gibraltar and to the administrative law such as the Companies Act, or legislation for the creation of new forms, or modifications to old forms acknowledge this principle and seek to protect it. It is important not to undermine the principle that 'form gives no benefit' and the administrative neutrality of the Income Tax Act 2010. Opportunities for avoidance arise from provisions being amended in isolation to the rest of our law. Tax law does not sit in isolation to all other forms of law, there are no types of law which are entirely irrelevant to tax. The law is not a series of silos that function in isolation to each other, it is a single piece of cloth knitted together from the strands of legislation; change one thing in one place and a number of other provisions will be effected.

A good example of well-made law in this area is the Limited Liability

130 The particular examples given are a result of the interplay of ss 11 – 13, 18 and Schedule 1 Table C of the Income Tax Act 2010.

Partnerships Act 2009 which (at s12)[131] specifically deals with the taxation treatment of LLPs: nothing is left to chance, no presumed understanding is required, and with that the principles of the taxation system are preserved. We would hope that this example can be followed in the coming years to ensure novel provisions are similarly understood by those drafting them in their context.

131 s12 Limited Liability Partnerships Act 2009

Chapter 4

WORK IS TAXABLE, WEALTH IS NOT

The Principle of Taxing Behavioural Outcomes

T Rosado-Standen and J Bear

Income can be defined as money that an individual or a business receives either by providing a service, goods or through investment. The concept of taxing income has its roots in ancient civilizations, with the earliest records concerning its collection dating back to Egypt in 1580 BC.[132] One of the first countries to adopt a law governing income tax was England in 1799, when imposing what was described as a temporary tax on income to help pay the costs of the Napoleonic Wars, a tax which was accepted as a vital price for winning the war against Napoleon. [133] This temporary tax was repealed in 1815 but would be adopted again in 1842. Income tax has remained since this time, but in the UK retains its 'temporary' nature in that it requires annual review by Parliament. Numerous other countries around the world adopted forms of income tax through the 19th and 20th centuries, examples being the United States in 1861, Italy in 1864, India in 1886, Spain in 1902 and Canada in 1917.[134]

In 1830, when Gibraltar became a Crown Colony, there was no local representation and the city's affairs, including the levying of import duties and rates,

---

132 Charles R Metzger, 'Brief History of Income Taxation' [1927] 13(11) American Bar Association Journal [Online] 662-667 (Last accessed on 26th February 2024). Available from http://www.jstor.org/stable/25707292

133 Please see further: https://www.parliament.uk/about/living-heritage/transforming-society/private-lives/taxation/overview/incometax/ (Last accessed on 26th February 2024).

134 Charles R Metzger, 'Brief History of Income Taxation' [1927] 13(11) American Bar Association Journal [Online] 662-667. Available from http://www.jstor.org/stable/25707292 (Last accessed on 26th February 2024).

were handled by the Colonial Office in London. In the early twentieth century, the policy of the Colonial Office became one of gradually introducing a degree of self-government in all Crown territories. The first elections for a City Council in Gibraltar were held in 1921, but the gradual increase in local representation halted with the outbreak of the Second World War. Post-war, the pace of reform increased, thanks to the work of the Transport and General Workers' Union and the first members of the Association for the Advancement of Civil Rights, led by Sir Joshua Hassan.[135] The post war settlement which led to the creation of the welfare state across Europe meant that states everywhere were subject to greater demands than ever, a now more autonomous Gibraltarian state required greater funds and as a result an income tax was levied in Gibraltar for the first time by the 1952 Act.[136]

Wealth Based Taxes

In addition to taxes on income, states commonly levy taxes on wealth and capital. These include wealth tax, inheritance tax (or estate duties), gift tax and capital gains tax. In Gibraltar, estate duty was introduced under the Estate Duties Ordinance in 1934. During the Gibraltar 1996 general election campaign, the Gibraltar Social Democrats ('GSD') manifested a commitment to abolish estate duty between spouses and reduce the rate of estate duty between next of kin. The GSD's 1996 manifesto states:

> 'Taxes payable on death are usually paid only by those who have not made arrangements to avoid it. These are usually those who can least afford it. It is particularly harsh as a tax that applies between husband and wife. It is wrong that savings made by married people for the welfare of their spouses upon their death should be taxed. The GSD will in the first term of office abolish estate duty between spouses. We will also review estate duty levels and allowances with regard to inheritance between net of kin'.[137]

---

135 W.G.F Jackson,., F.J Cantos,. *From Fortress to Democracy: The Political Biography of Sir Joshua Hassan*. Gibraltar Books Ltd (1995).

136 Income Tax Act 1952

137 Gibraltar Social Democrats 1996 Manifesto, page 9

After being elected to Government, in 1997 the GSD upheld this commitment, but went a step further in abolishing estate duty in its entirety. The following reasons were submitted before the House of Assembly (which would subsequently become the Gibraltar Parliament in 2007):

> The amount that would be collected (once the tax no longer applied between husbands and wives) would no longer be worth the administrative effort and resources needed to collect the tax effectively and efficiently;
>
> The amounts collected in recent years showed that it was rare for estates to be subjected to the full rigour of the tax; and
>
> It was unfair: a straightforward matter for wealthier individuals to plan their affairs around estate duty, whilst those bequeathed smaller estates, from people who had worked their whole lives, were more likely to be subjected to the tax.[138]
>
> In fact, aside from the year 1993/1994, which was extraordinary due to the value of one particular estate, the figures of recent years before the abolition of the tax were low[139]:

Year	Collections
1991/2	£67,000
1992/3	£85,000
1993/4	£583,000
1994/5	£108,000
1995/6	£194,000
1996/7	£40,000

Estate duty was subsequently abolished, on the basis that the tax was not raising significant revenue for the Government, that it was individuals with more modest estates who were being most subjected to the tax, and at the time Gibraltar's anti-avoidance tax measures were unsophisticated. In the then House of Assembly it was specifically noted that the abolition of estate duty was justified due to the relatively small amounts collected. A comparison was made with the previous

138 Gibraltar House of Assembly, Hansard 26th June 1997 (adj to 22nd July 1997), page 12

139 Ibid

year, in which an increase in personal allowances had produced a loss of nearly £2 million of revenue for the Government.[140]

Capital Gains Tax ('CGT') is a more recent form of taxation levied on gains realised on the disposal of assets. An early adopter of the tax was the United States. After the 16th Amendment to the Constitution was enacted in 1913, Congress was provided with 'the power to lay and collect taxes on incomes from whatever source derived, without appropriation'[141]. The US Revenue Act of 1913 followed by those of 1916, 1918 and 1921 defined and standardised the way taxes were levied on profits, with the 1921 Act making the distinction between income, gains from capital assets that were held for less than two years, and those held for more than two years.[142] This action was in response to concerns that the combination of capital gains and income tax were discouraging economic growth, particularly that the combination of the two taxes had peaked at 77% during World War One.[143]

In the UK, a comprehensive capital gains tax was first introduced in 1965 under Harold Wilson's Government, by the then Labour Chancellor James Callaghan who said '[t]here is little dispute nowadays that capital gains confer much the same kind of benefit on the recipient as taxed earnings more hardly won. Yet earnings pay tax in full while capital gains go free' [144]. There was a perception that the tax system was unfair because businesses and individuals could make significant profits from the sale of assets without being subject to the same level of taxation as those who earned a regular income. His conclusion was that a capital gains tax would remove the incentive of the 'skilful manipulator' to engage in avoidance by converting taxable income into capital.[145]

Gibraltar, on the other hand, for reasons examined below, has never taxed

140 Ibid

141 The 16th Amendment, March 15, 1913; Ratified Amendments, 1795-1992; General Records of the United States Government; Record Group 11; National Archives

142 Anita Wells, 'Legislative History of Treatment of Capital Gains Under the Federal Income Tax, 1913-1948' [1949] National Tax Journal 2, no.1 <http://www.jstor.org/stable/41789799> (Last accessed on 26th February 2024)

143 Anita Wells, 'Legislative History of Treatment of Capital Gains Under the Federal Income Tax, 1913-1948' [1949] National Tax Journal 2, no.1 <http://www.jstor.org/stable/41789799> (Last accessed on 26th February 2024)

144 HC Deb 6 April 1965 Series 5 Vol. 710 C 245

145 Ibid

capital. Though the boundary between income and capital is a complex which is not defined in legislation.

The Charge of Tax

Today in Gibraltar, ordinarily resident individuals are taxed on all income generated by a trade, business or vocation on a worldwide basis. In contrast, the Gibraltar corporate taxation system is a territorial taxation system, which charges tax in accordance with Section 11(1) of the Income Act 2010 ('ITA').

Section 11(1) states that:

> Tax shall, subject to the provisions of this Act and of the Rules, be payable at the rate or rates specified from time to time for each year of assessment or accounting period upon the income specified in tables A to C inclusive of Schedule 1 accruing in or derived from Gibraltar of any person.

Companies in Gibraltar are thus taxed on a territorial basis, meaning that they are only taxed on income which is accrued and derived in Gibraltar (subject to a few exceptions which lie beyond the scope of this Chapter). Gibraltar only taxes income; it has no CGT, inheritance tax, wealth tax, gift taxes, VAT or tax on bank interest.

It is not that capital gains taxes are 'exempt' from Gibraltar's tax base, but rather that the tax base, born from the Model Colonial Territories Income Tax Ordinance of 1922,[146] was never designed to accommodate CGT to begin with:

> 'All outgoings and expenses wholly and exclusively incurred in the production of income should be allowed as deductions in computing the amount of a person's "chargeable income". On the other hand, no deduction should be admitted for expenditure of a domestic or private character or for capital

146 Great Britain. Inter-Departmental Committee on Income Tax in the Colonies Not Possessing Responsible Government, 'Report of the Inter-Departmental Committee on Income Tax in the Colonies Not Possessing Responsible Government' (London: H.M Stationery Off., 1922)

expenditure.'[147]

Gibraltar may seem to be the outlier now, at least in European terms, but it is the tax bases of other jurisdictions that have changed around it and provided for CGT, not Gibraltar that has deliberately 'diverged'. Unlike those jurisdictions that have deliberately designed their system to attract foreign inward investment Gibraltar has simply remained the same. Indeed, it is important to appreciate that there is a gap between what is 'exempted' from the tax base and what lies within its 'scope of taxation'.

In order to appreciate this gap, an understanding of a jurisdiction's broader sociocultural and economic context is crucial.[148] Tax bases are neither constructed nor operational in a vacuum, but are rather part of the complex web of social, cultural, economic and political strands of the jurisdiction in which they sit. We must understand the wider system in which they operate and in which tax structures evolve. Any assessment is always context driven: a tax system which worked well in one given time period may not be appropriate in another.[149] Equally, a tax system which can be hung comfortably upon one sociocultural and economic framework may not be hung comfortably upon another.

As Murphy and Nagel argue, something can become so embedded in a social structure that we take it to be the 'norm' or even 'the natural order' of things',[150] but it does not follow that it is, particularly when we realise that we form a metric based on our own standpoint, the standpoint of the system of which we are a part. Necessarily, smaller jurisdictions may form different reference systems to their economically complex neighbours. Gibraltar, of course, is a small jurisdiction, beset with its own idiosyncrasies.

Whilst a full analysis of Gibraltar's socioeconomic history is beyond the scope of this Chapter, it is crucial to orientate the tax base within its broad context. With

---

147 ibid, p7

148 Grahame Jackson and Harriet Brown, 'The role of context in interpreting international tax instruments: a solution to the erosion of internal cohesion of domestic tax systems by international law? The EU Directive on Administrative Cooperation Version 6 (DAC6) – a case study' [2022] Bulletin for International Taxation

149 The Mirrlees Review, *Tax by Design* (OUP 2011)

150 Liam Murphy and Thomas Nagel., *The Myth of Ownership: Taxes and Justice*, (OUP 2002)

the closure of the land frontier with Spain in 1969, of which there had been signs for a number of years preceding the eventual closure, Gibraltar had to find ways to reinvent itself and remain sufficiently internationally competitive to attract the income which it could not self-produce. Whilst during the intervening period Gibraltar was highly dependent on the income received from the notable presence of Ministry of Defence forces on the Rock, it was in the 1990s that the territory rebuilt its identity as a financial centre. In order to attract the external investment, Gibraltar needed to ensure that there were tax incentives, or at least to minimise the disincentives. However, whilst such income is crucial to Gibraltar's economy, it should also be appreciated that Gibraltar enjoys a number of other significant income streams, most notably bunkering — the supply of fuel to ships — and tourism.

Even prior to this 'campaign' in the 1990s to revive Gibraltar's image and economy, Gibraltar had strived to be attractive, for tax purposes, to the external income it hoped to attract, and had operated a system of 'exempt companies'. [151] Gibraltar had based the concept on the IBC (International Business Companies) model of the Caribbean jurisdictions, which sprang up in the 1960s and 1970s.[152] This had resulted in a two-tier system of corporate taxation for companies in Gibraltar: a normal rate of 35% for regular Gibraltar companies, and a complete exemption for those companies awarded the required licence. Under the Companies (Taxation and Concessions) Act 1983, 'exempt' companies had to meet certain requirements including that it did not carry out any trade in Gibraltar, and that no Gibraltarian or Gibraltar resident held any interest in the company. As the century drew to a close, the exempt company regime came under pressure from the EU as it was at odds with their state aid rules and a Commission decision[153] resulted in the abolition of the last exempt company in 2010. Eventually, Gibraltar adjusted its tax system to move towards a lower rate of corporate tax. At the same time, as is discussed in later sections of this Chapter, further changes to the tax landscape were underway.

Gibraltar is not a fully sovereign state, though it may well meet some of the

151 Companies (Taxation and Concessions) 1983

152 International Business Company: Offshore IBC What is it & Benefits (offshore-protection.com), accessed 26th July 2023

153 State Aid E 7/2002 (ex C53/2001 & NN52/2000) – United Kingdom Proposal for appropriate measures under Article 88(1) of the EC Treaty concerning Gibraltar exempt companies, accessed 26th July 2023

definitions of 'state' in use[154] and as such it lacks a number of categories of expense that are faced by larger, more sovereign states. For example, it does not maintain a navy, it has no nuclear power stations, nor an extensive pool of unemployed people, nor does it contribute to a space programme nor does it hold international summits. This gives rise to a reduced need for income, since the Gibraltarian state just does less than its larger neigbours, and as a consequence it can operate itself with a lower tax burden and a lower national debt. This means that it has not been necessary to scope out additional sources of revenue by levying more taxes and expanding the tax base. Even post-Pandemic, Gibraltar has maintained a healthy debt to GDP ratio. For 2021/2022, Gibraltar's estimated overall Government Revenue was £633 million, whilst estimated net public debt stood at over £558 million as of 31st March 2021, and its nominal GDP that year was estimated at £2.4 billion. That set Gibraltar's level of debt at approximately 25.6% of its estimated GDP in 2021/22.[155]

A comparison with the UK's figures serves to emphasise the different contexts in which the jurisdictions are situated. At the end of Quarter 1 of 2022 (January to March), the general government gross debt for the United Kingdom stood at an estimated £2,365.4 billion, 99.6% of its GDP.[156] A country with such debt will be driven to raise revenue, and a widened tax base is one obvious means to achieve this.

In his 2022 Budget Address,[157] the Chief Minister of Gibraltar maintained that increases in Government revenue during his Party's time in office (which commenced in 2011), have not been driven by taxation. This would lend weight to the fact that Gibraltar has no need to widen the tax base, such that if they did, they would be breaching the implicit principle of taxing only what is necessary. Indeed, it is a generally accepted principle of tax policy that a taxation should be limited in

154 See Tse-shyang Chen, F. (2001). 'The Meaning of States in the Membership Provisions of the United Nations Charter', Indiana International and Comparative Law Review Vol 12, No1 2001

155 Please see further: https://www.gibraltar.gov.gi/uploads/files/public-finances/SUMMARY%20OF%20PUBLIC%20FINANCES%20-%20web.pdf (Last accessed on 26th February 2024).

156 UK government debt and deficit - Office for National Statistics (ons.gov.uk)

157 Please see further: https://www.gibraltar.gov.gi/uploads/449-2022.pdf (Last accessed on 26th February 2024).

scope and remain free of excess and unnecessary taxes.[158]

Accordingly, from the perspective of a jurisdiction where the tax base includes CGT[159], a limited tax base such as Gibraltar's may seem to be a 'deviation' from the norm. It is not, capital gains have always been outside of the tax base, as is consumption of goods and services (there is no VAT); this is a difference, not a deviance.

The Meaning of 'Profits or Gains'

Having given some reasons for Gibraltar's tax base being as it is and setting it in its socio-economic context, we will now turn to a legal analysis of that tax base. As previously established, Gibraltar's corporate tax regime is governed by section 11 ITA 2010. This section directs us to Schedule 1 of the Act which contains the Heads of Charge. At Table A, we find the following language:

> 'the profits or gains of a company, a foundation or a trust from any trade, business, profession or vocation'

This explicitly ties the 'profits or gains' generated to the trade which generates them, and not to any source of a capital nature.

The Badges of Trade Test

When considering the taxation system applicable to companies, the basic position is that the primary head of charge is that of 'the profits or gains of a trade business profession or vocation'. [160] Given this the question 'how can it be determined whether a transaction gives rise to trading income or a capital receipt?' is central

158 Robert F. van Brederode, *Political Philosophy and Taxation: A History from the Enlightenment to the Present*, (Springer 2022), p207

159 Which as explained has been a relatively recent innovation in many developed economies

160 In the case of passive income this is extended to include intercompany interest, royalties and non-trade income from moveable property.

to the Gibraltar taxation system.

Given the limited number of Gibraltar tax related cases in the domestic system, we are obliged to look to the English courts for persuasive case law. The English courts have developed a series of tests, or so-called 'badges', to decide whether an activity revolves around trade or around capital ventures.

It was the case of *Marson (H M Inspector of Taxes) v Morton and Others* [1986] STC 463 which set out the principles that have come to be used in assessing whether or not a transaction bears the 'badges of trade'. However, the Judge in this case was careful to emphasise that the test ought to be taken as a set of guiding principles, as opposed to a conclusive 'tick-box' test, and should be considered holistically, with no one badge being definitive of trade in isolation:

> 'I emphasise again that the matters I have mentioned are not a comprehensive list and no single item is in any way decisive. I believe that in order to reach a proper factual assessment in each case it is necessary to stand back, having looked at those matters, and look at the whole picture and ask the question - and for this purpose it is no bad thing to go back to the words of the statute - was this an adventure in the nature of trade? In some cases perhaps more homely language might be appropriate by asking the question, was the taxpayer investing the money or was he doing a deal?'[161]

The 'badges', which we shall explore in greater detail below, may be summarised as follows:

i. The presence or absence of a profit-seeking motive
ii. The number of transactions
iii. The nature of the asset
iv. The existence of similar trading transactions or interests
v. Changes to the asset
vi. The way the sale was carried out
vii. The source of finance
viii. The interval of time between purchase and sale
ix. The method of acquisition

161 *Marson (H M Inspector of Taxes) v Morton and Others* [1986] 1 WLR 1343 STC 463

i. The presence or absence of a profit-seeking motive

An intention to make a profit will generally support trading, but is not in itself conclusive, and as with the other badges needs to be considered in relation to the other elements of the guiding principles. The taxpayer needs to prove the motive, rather than the existence of profit, to establish the carrying-on of a trade. If the acquisition of an investment was to realise a profit, or a commercial motive, it is likely to amount to trade. Speculation, however, does not amount to intention to make a profit, especially where the risk was recognised by the taxpayer and the investment or project nevertheless pursued.

ii. The number of transactions

If a transaction is carried out on a single occasion, it is unlikely that it will be treated as indicative of carrying on a trade. On the other hand, if the transactions are systematically repeated, particularly at a high frequency, this will support 'trade' (*Pickford v Quirke CA 1927, 13 TC 251*). However, cases will be taken on their own merits. In the case of *Salt v Chamberlain* [1979] 53 TC143, a number of Stock Exchange transactions (200 sales and purchases over a three-year period) was not sufficient to establish that the taxpayer was trading due to the nature of the transaction. On the other hand, a single transaction undertaken, such as a purchase of a commodity at a volume which surpasses that required for personal use, and a subsequent resale of this large quantity of commodity, as in the case of *CIR v Fraser* [1942] 24TC498), may be deemed to amount to trade. In this case, Mr Fraser, a woodcutter, had bought a consignment of whisky in bond and sold it through an agent at a profit. In concluding that the purchase amounted to trade, the court considered two factors. Firstly, that it was of a quantity far in excess of what an individual could be expected to consume. Secondly, and related to the above, it was deemed to offer no 'pride of possession'[162], i.e. there was no obvious enjoyment that was likely to be experienced as a result of the individual's purchase, unlike, for example, a work of art, or a quantity of whisky more commensurate with personal consumption.

iii. The nature of the asset

162 Pride of possession is a phrase which is used to delineate the pleasure to be had simply from owning an asset. Such as the joy one has from a new car rather than an old one.

Is the asset of such a type or quantity that it can only be turned to advantage by a sale? Or did it yield an income or give 'pride of possession'? An example of the latter would be a piece of art for personal enjoyment.

However, problems may arise when assets are combined such as:

- Investments with the ability to generate income;
- Personal assets; or
- Some assets used by a trade, such as plant and machinery.

In *Marson v Morton* [1986] 1 WLR 1343, land was purchased with the intention to hold it as an investment. The land did not have planning permission, and no income was generated by the land. The land was later sold following an unsolicited offer. The transaction was far-removed from the taxpayer's usual trade as a potato merchant, thus was treated as an investment, rather than trading profit.

iv. The existence of similar trading transaction or interests

Transactions that are similar to those of an existing trade may themselves qualify as trading. Further, it should be considered whether the particular transaction is similar to the ordinary business of the taxpayer in question. For example, a one-off sale of a tractor by a farmer is more likely to be considered to be a trade transaction than such a sale by an accountant.

The case of *CIR v Fraser* [1942] 24TC498, as discussed above, best illustrates this badge:

> 'The purchaser of a large quantity of a quantity of a commodity like whisky, greatly in excess of what could be used by himself, his family and friends, a commodity which yields no pride of possession, which cannot be turned to account except by a process of realisation, I can scarcely consider to be other than an adventurer in a transaction in the nature of a trade... Most important of all, the actual dealings of the respondent with the whisky were exactly of the kind that take place in ordinary trade.'[163]

v. Changes to the asset

If you buy a product with the intention to modify it to make it more attractive for

163 *CIR v Fraser* [1942] 24TC498

sale, it is possible that this may be found to amount to trading. Moreover, the court may look at whether the item purchased was resold in one lot as it was bought, or whether it was broken down into saleable lots. If it was broken down, this is again some indication that it was a trading transaction, the purchase being with a view to resell at profit by carrying out a modification in relation to the object bought.

Cape Brandy Syndicate v CIR [1921] 2KB 403 was concerned with members of a wine syndicate who joined in a separate syndicate to purchase brandy from South Africa. Some of the brandy was shipped to the East, with the remainder sent to London to be blended with French brandy, re-casked and sold at a profit. The taxpayer sought to make the case that the transaction was of a capital nature arising from the sale of an investment. However, it was ultimately held that a trade was being carried out and so the income was assessable as trading profit.

vi. The way the sale was carried out

Was the asset sold in a way that was typical of trading organisations? Alternatively, did it have to be sold to raise cash for an emergency?

According to the HMRC guidance, it is always a positive indicator of this badge if a transaction follows that of an 'undisputed trade'. In *CIR v Livingston* and others [1926] 11TC538, three unconnected individuals bought a cargo vessel together. The vessel was converted into a steam-drifter and sold for profit. The purchase was the first vessel which the individuals had bought. An assessment was raised on the profit which was upheld as a trading profit. The judge stated that:

> 'I think the test, which must be used to determine whether a venture such as we are now considering is, or is not, in the nature of "trade", is whether the operations involved in it are of the same kind, and carried on in the same way, as those which are characteristic of ordinary trading in the line of business in which the venture was made.'[164]

vii. The source of finance

The court will consider whether money was borrowed to buy the asset, and whether the funds could only be repaid by selling the asset.

Where a short-term loan has been taken out to fund the asset, HMRC are likely to find that the asset was specifically purchased with a view to selling it. In

164 *CIR v Livingstone* [1926] 11TC538

Wisdom v Chamberlain [1968] 45TC92, silver bullion was purchased on a short-term loan. Mr Wisdom could not service the interest payments from his existing money, but as soon as he sold the bullion and repaid the loan, he found he had made a substantial profit. The profit was found to be taxable as trading income.

viii. The interval of time between purchase and sale

Assets that are the subject of trade will normally, albeit not in all cases, be sold quickly. On the other hand, if you have owned an asset for a long time, it is easier to argue that it was purchased for 'pride of possession' and personal consumption. It follows that an intention to resell an asset shortly after purchase will support the distinction of trading. On the other hand, an asset which is to be held indefinitely is much less likely to be a subject of trade.

ix. The method of acquisition

Finally, we must turn to the way in which the asset has been acquired. An asset that is inherited, or acquired as a gift, is unlikely to be the subject of trade, although of course, there could always be exceptions.

In the case of *Taylor v Good* [1974] 1 All ER 1137, a taxpayer purchased a house with the intention of using it as his family home. However, when his partner did not approve of the house and refused to move in, he was forced to immediately sell the house. The taxpayer had a genuine intention of using the property for the long-term purpose of a family home, and not simply buying it for a profit-making motive, such that the transaction was not deemed to be one of trade. However, the Judge was careful, again, to highlight the nuances of the Badges of Trade, acknowledging that there could be occasions where a profit-making motive is formed later:

> 'Even if the house was purchased with no thought of trading, I do not see why an intention to trade could not be formed later. What is bought or otherwise acquired (for example, under a will) with no thought of trading cannot thereby acquire an immunity so that, however filled with the desire and intention of trading the owner may later become, it can never be said that any transaction by him with the property constitutes trading. For the taxpayer a non-trading inception may be a valuable asset: but it is no palladium. The proposition that an initial intention not to trade may be displaced by a subsequent intention, in the course of the ownership of the property in question, is, I think, sufficiently

established...'[165]

The Non-allowance of Capital Deductions

It would seem entirely logical that in an income-only tax system capital expenditure is not permissible as an expense or deduction against income profits. However, Gibraltar does have a limited capital allowances regime which allows capital expenditure on certain classes of assets to a limited degree and in a regulated fashion. This is a reflection of the fact that some capital expenditure is a necessary prerequisite for the generation of any income. The regime is very limited in its nature compared to other jurisdictions.

In Gibraltar, the following capital allowances are currently available at the date of writing (June 2023):

- A 'first year allowance' for the first £30,000 of qualifying expenditure on plant and machinery (including fixtures and fittings), and the first £50,000 of qualifying expenditure on computer equipment;
- Thereafter, qualifying assets are pooled and subject to an annual capital, or wear and tear, allowance. Allowances of 15% are available for plant and machinery, computer equipment and motor vehicles, calculated on a reducing-balance basis;
- Capital allowance for industrial buildings is deductible at the rate of 4% per annum on a straight line basis.

Essentially, capital allowances are tax-deductible expenses which are available in respect of qualifying capital expenditure. Capital expenditure are funds used by the company to acquire, upgrade, and maintain physical assets, such as the purchase of property or plant and equipment. Capital expenditure typically amounts to a one-off large purchase of fixed assets that will be used to support generating income over a longer period.

To assist in conceiving of the difference between capital expenditure and income expense, we may draw on an often-used analogy between a tree and its fruit.

A capital item may be likened to a tree: the one-off fixed asset. On the other

165 *Taylor v Good* [1974] All ER 1137

hand, income expenditure is typically an ongoing operating expense, in the form of short-term expenses that are used in running the daily operations of the business. This expenditure is the cost of pruning and watering the tree so it may bear fruit. Without the tree, fruit could not grow.[166] Ultimately, capital expenditure is required for the production of income, so that the trade can operate. Effectively, capital allowances enable cost recovery, allowing businesses to recover the costs of their investments, and to facilitate their business activity (the growth of the fruit). Nevertheless, the capital investment has a value in itself: a capital value.

The principle of income tax, as we have seen, is that there is only deduction permitted for expenditure incurred wholly and exclusively in the generation of the income in question. Thus, a capital allowance regime would allow a deduction of capital expenses, with their capital value, where there is no corresponding inclusion in the form of CGT.

Tax is double-ended. There ought only to be deductions where there is a corresponding inclusion, in order to avoid creating a situation similar to what is technically known as 'mismatch', as further detailed in Chapter 6. Were Gibraltar to have a broad capital allowances regime in the absence of CGT, such a mismatch would result due to the existence of an allowance for capital expenditure without the matching deduction of CGT. However, in order to stimulate economic growth, some capital allowances need to be granted, but only to such an extent that the income-only tax-base is not violated. Thus, having a very limited capital allowances regime provides that necessary stimulus, whilst preserving the integrity of the income-only tax system.[167]

No Wealth Tax

Wealth tax is a broad-based tax on the ownership of net wealth. It is a tax levied on all (or most) of the assets owned by an individual. Net wealth is a person's assets

166 However, the tree-fruit analogy has its limits, as was identified in the South African case *Visser v CIR* SATC 271: 'for what is in principle or tree in the hands of one man may be interest or fruit in the hands of another. Law books in the hands of a lawyer are a capital asset; in the hands of a bookseller they are a trade asset'

167 It is worthy of note that there is a claw-back provision contained in Schedule 3 Part 2 Chapter III para 4 of the ITA 2010 that goes someway to resolving this issue.

minus their debts.[168] A primary aim of jurisdictions which have imposed wealth taxes is to shift the burden of tax towards more affluent households.[169] Gibraltar does not levy wealth tax. Wealth tax is not generally part of the UK's tradition either, however, the UK has debated its implementation on numerous occasions, notably in times of public finance crisis. It is worth analysing the reasons why it was considered and ultimately rejected, so that we can draw a comparison with the position in Gibraltar.

After the Second World War, it was Cambridge-educated economist, Nicholas Kaldor, who first recommended the implementation of a wealth tax in the UK. [170] It was not until the 1974 general election that Harold Wilson's Labour Party made a manifesto commitment to implement such a tax. Before the election, the Labour Party had consented to implement a series of measures aimed at fundamentally redistributing income and wealth, to secure trade union agreement for wage restraint during a period of unsustainable inflation.[171]

The Labour Party Manifesto stated:

> 'Redistribute income and wealth. We shall introduce an annual Wealth Tax on the rich; bring in a new tax on major transfers of personal wealth; heavily tax speculation in property – including a new tax on property companies.'[172]

Despite election victory and the passing of a Green Paper, Labour eventually decided to abandon their pursuit of a wealth tax in 1976, in the face of scrutiny and disapproval, particularly from the recently established Institute for Fiscal Studies, Treasury officials and external groups.[173]

---

168 Advani, Chamberlain and Summers, Wealth Tax Commission, 'A Wealth Tax For the UK' 2020 p. 7

169 Scheuer, Florian, and Joel Slemrod. 'Taxing Our Wealth.' The Journal of Economic Perspectives, vol. 35, no. 1, 2021, pp. 207–30. JSTOR, https://www.jstor.org/stable/27008021. (Last accessed on 26th February 2024).

170 Glennerster, Howard (2012) 'Why was a wealth tax for the UK abandoned? Lessons for the policy process and tackling of wealth inequality.' Journal of Social Policy, 41 (2) pp.233-249. DOI: 10.1017/S0047279411000602

171 Ibid

172 United Kingdom Labour Party Manifesto 1974

173 Arun Advani., Helen Miller, and Andy Summers ('Taxes on wealth: Time for anoth-

Included among the objections for raising a wealth tax were the following:

a. That although the tax would remove major concentrations of wealth, it would produce much less revenue, as people instead give away wealth to family members and charities;
b. Opposition from external interests, such as bodies representing the owners of country houses, small businesses and the Bank of England; and
c. Concerns about the tax leading to capital flight, with businesses moving out of the UK and people seeking non-resident status.[174]

It is worth noting that despite these objections, the Meade Report, published by the Institute for Fiscal Studies in 1978 recommended an annual tax on the stock of wealth to supplement a system of taxes on consumption,[175] yet once again the prospect was not further pursued. In 2011, the Mirrlees Review re-examined and ultimately rejected the possibility of an annual wealth tax in the UK, concluding, with reference to experiences of implementing the tax in other jurisdictions, that it would be inefficient, unfair and costly to administer.[176]

The objections outlined above are similar to those raised in support of the GSD's abolition of estate duty in Gibraltar in 1996 (as discussed above). Moreover since 1996, Gibraltar's tax base has grown significantly.

For taxation to occur in Gibraltar, an activity or behaviour must have taken place. A taxable event can occur from income generated by one of the heads of charge as set out in tables A-C of schedule 1 of the ITA 2010. These are wide-ranging, from the profits or gains of an individual from self-employed work to royalties received by a company. Gibraltar also levies stamp duty, triggered by the transfer or sale of any Gibraltar property, shares in a company owning

---

er look?' [2021], Fiscal Studies, 42, pp. 389–395.

174 Howard Glennerster 'Why was a wealth tax for the UK abandoned?: lessons for the policy process and tackling of wealth inequality', [2012] 41(2) Journal of Social Policy, pp. 233-249

175 The Meade Committee, Report of the Committee on the Working of the Monetary System, Cmnd 6753 (HMSO 1978).

176 Arun Advani., Helen Miller, and Andy Summers, 'Taxes on wealth: Time for another look?' [2021], Fiscal Studies, 42, pp. 389–395.

Gibraltar real estate and on mortgages secured on Gibraltar property.[177] It is also worth mentioning that import duty is applicable to goods entering Gibraltar at varying rates. In all of the above examples, an event has to occur for the taxes to be triggered. In Gibraltar, tax is not triggered by passive occurrences or events, for example an annual charge on an individual's net wealth or an inheritance that they have received. In other words Gibraltar taxes the outcomes of behaviours, not wealth in itself. In this it mirrors the British tradition.

Although wealth tax is not currently part of Gibraltar's tax system, could it be? In modern times, a move away from wealth tax has been prevalent. In the 1990s, for example, twelve OECD member countries levied an annual wealth tax. Now however, all but three of those countries (Norway, Spain and Switzerland) have repealed this tax.[178] Decisions for repeal have centred around efficiency and administrative concerns, low revenue collection and the conclusion that net wealth taxes have frequently failed to meet their redistributive goals.[179]

Furthermore, in July 2020, Rishi Sunak, then Chancellor of the Exchequer, was quoted as stating that he believed that there would never be a right time for a wealth tax.[180] Despite this recent move away from wealth taxes, however, the Covid-19 Pandemic and its resulting strain on public finances, has caused a number of jurisdictions to look for ways to recover funds and to consider whether a wealth tax should be introduced.

One example of this is Argentina, which in December 2020 passed a new one-off levy on citizens with assets over $2.5 million, to pay for resources to assist with the covid-19 Pandemic.[181] In the UK, a group of academics known as the Wealth

177 Stamp Duties Act 2005,Schedule 1

178 Arun Advani, Helen Miller and Andy Summers, 'Taxes on wealth: Time for another look?' [2021], Fiscal Studies, 42, pp. 389–395.

179 'The Role and Design of Net Wealth Taxes in the OECD' – (12 th April 2018), – available online on: https://www.oecd-ilibrary.org/taxation/the-role-and-design-of-net-wealth-taxes-in-the-oecd_9789264290303-en?itemId=/content/publication/9789264290303-en&_csp_=b746b256f23e109b9244f92078eb7093&itemIGO=oecd&itemContentType=book (Last accessed on 26th February 2024).

180 Arun Advani, Emma Chamberlain and Andy Summers, 'A Wealth Tax For the UK', (Wealth Tax Commission, 2020), pp. 5

181 Arun Advani, Helen Miller and Andy Summers, 'Taxes on wealth: Time for another look?' [2021], Fiscal Studies, 42, pp. 389–395.

Tax Commission delivered a final report on whether a wealth tax should be introduced. The Commission endorsed a one-off wealth tax instead of an annual levy, which they projected could raise at least 260 billion pounds if it consisted of a flat rate of 5% on assets over £500,000.

At the time of writing, the EU Tax Observatory had just published a proposal for a Global Minimum Wealth Tax for those ultra-high net worth individuals worth in excess of £1,000,000,000. However, it has not yet gained significant support.[182]

Conclusion

If Gibraltar introduced taxes on wealth it would be a major departure from the design of the Gibraltar taxation system as it exists at the time of writing, both practically and conceptually. Ultimately, tax systems are not operative in a vacuum, but evolve within a complex web of sociocultural, economic and political factors.

Gibraltar's situation is unique: as a very small territory it must remain sufficiently internationally competitive to attract the income which it cannot self-produce. Propelled by the hardship experienced from the closed frontier with Spain in the latter half of the 20th century, Gibraltar improved its self-sufficiency by developing as a finance centre and attracting external investment. The introduction of the Category 2 status for individuals with a net-worth of over £2 million (discussed further in Chapter 3) was aimed at injecting private capital into the jurisdiction. Furthermore, with a small population and therefore limited workforce, the introduction of the HEPSS status (High Executive Possessing Specialist Skills) aims to encourage individuals possessing specialist skills to relocate to Gibraltar and fill in talent-gaps where such talent is not locally available.

Finally, it is an implicit principle of tax morality that a jurisdiction should not tax more than is necessary. With relatively low demands on its exchequer and as a result a low national debt to GDP ratio, Gibraltar has not needed to expand its tax base to include CGT or wealth taxes in the way that many other jurisdictions have, and so long as this remains the case, it should not.

The intellectually coherent taxation system which was instituted for the requirements of a growing trading colony in the 1950s remains intact and fit

182 Global Tax Evasion Report 2024, EU Tax Observatory (2023)

for purpose. It has produced sufficient revenue in all but the most exceptional circumstances. It is our opinion that Gibraltar has the taxation system it needs. In respect of companies, it taxes trading activity and a number of forms of passive income. The exempt company and the anomalies that regime created have been abolished. The Gibraltar system remains that the outcome of trade and other active behaviours are taxable, wealth itself is not.

Chapter 5

A MEMBER OF THE INTERNATIONAL COMMUNITY

The Principle of Integration of International Obligations

David Montegriffo and Louise Federico

Introduction / Abstract

The story of modern Gibraltar on the world stage is that of a committed and compliant participant within the international community. As explored in this chapter, Gibraltar complies with its obligations and has implemented various international tax regimes in line with global moves towards increased transparency and cross-border information exchange.

Historical context and the shift 'onshore'

In terms of setting the scene, it is worth considering Gibraltar's progress over the last 25 years, from a jurisdiction firmly positioned in the 'offshore' world to one standing together with the majority of large economies in being pivoted towards transparency and international co-operation.

Efforts by the international community to clamp down on tax avoidance and tax evasion have shaped the development of global tax frameworks, which in turn feed into the legal structures of compliant jurisdictions. There has been a focus on ensuring that these legal structures reduce the possibilities for internationally-mobile individuals and multi-national businesses to organise their tax affairs in ways which limit the sums payable. The desire to reform the international tax framework has been largely driven by larger and more powerful nations. Since 1996, the G7 countries have urged the Organisation for Economic Cooperation and Development (the OECD) to develop measures against tax regimes which might be exploited to harm their national tax bases. At the 1996 Lyon Summit, the following paragraph was included in their communiqué:

> 'Finally, globalisation is creating new challenges in the field of tax policy. Tax schemes aimed at attracting financial and other geographically mobile activities can create harmful tax competition between States, carrying risks of distorting trade and investment and could lead to the erosion of national tax bases. We strongly urge the OECD to vigorously pursue its work in this field, aimed at establishing a multilateral approach under which countries could operate individually and collectively to limit the extent of these practises. We will follow closely the progress on work by the OECD which is due to produce a report by 1998.'[183]

These moves marked the beginning of a global shift, away from the secretive 1990s world of offshore finance to today's era of transparency and information exchange. Following the release of the OECD's 1998 report 'Harmful Tax Competition: an emerging global issue' and the introduction of a blacklist system in its 2000 review 'Towards Global Tax Cooperation' (collectively the 'OECD Reports'), Gibraltar found itself branded as a 'tax haven' and listed in the initial iteration of the organisation's blacklist.[184] The OECD Reports introduced the threat of 'defensive measures' to be meted out against uncooperative jurisdictions which persist in harmful tax practices.

The threat of defensive measures which would place the viability of Gibraltar's strong financial sector at risk was, and remains, an intolerable proposition for the territory. It is especially important to consider these threats in the context of Gibraltar's history and geopolitical standing[185]. As Jackson (2023) highlights, 'it

183 G7 Lyon Summit Economic Communiqué, 28 June 1996

184 p17 OECD, 'Towards Global Tax Co-operation: Progress in Identifying and Eliminating Harmful Tax Practices' OECD Publishing 2000

185 In addition to the lingering presence of Spain's territorial claims and Gibraltar's desire for global recognition of its legitimacy and right to self-determination, politicians (and the rest of the local community) would have regard to the shift taking place in Gibraltar by the early 2000s, away from an historic economic dependence on the UK Ministry of Defence towards a solid economy based on financial services, shipping and tourism. These matters are touched upon in further detail in Chapter 8.

had long been the policy of the Gibraltar Government to ensure that Gibraltar was not a drag on the British Exchequer because a Britain which was suffering loss in its relationship with Gibraltar would be less likely to robustly defend Gibraltar against the territorial claim from Spain'.[186] Further, as indicated by Azopardi (2001), 'if a community is not self-sufficient it runs the risk of its aspirations being curtailed by extraneous factors that subjugate political wishes to economic realities'[187]. Gibraltar's continued economic viability is therefore an existential matter which, if mishandled, could severely hamper the territory's ability to pursue its political aspirations unburdened and with conviction.

It was against the menacing backdrop of OECD 'defensive measures' that in his New Year's message of 1st January 2001, the Chief Minister of Gibraltar Sir Peter Caruana stated:

> 'No one in Gibraltar... should underestimate how important the Finance Centre is to the economic, and therefore to the social and political prosperity, and indeed survival, of Gibraltar... Government will be obliged to take certain measures, especially changes to our tax system, to enable the Finance Centre to continue to flourish.[188]'

Gibraltar's blacklisting was also followed up in 2001 by the launch of an EU investigation which challenged the legality of Gibraltar's Tax-Exempt Company regime and Qualifying Company Regime in light of the State Aid Rules which flow from what is now Article 107 of the Treaty of the Functioning of the European Union. This was part of a wider in-depth investigation into 15 harmful tax practices across 12 member states, aimed at eliminating such exemptions.[189]

---

186 Jackson, Grahame, 'Understanding the Beps and Other OECD Tax Initiatives Including the Inclusive Framework in the Context of Treaties and State Inequality' (July 6, 2023). Journal of Tax Administration, Forthcoming , Available at SSRN: https://ssrn.com/abstract=4502101 (Last accessed on 26th February 2024)

187 Azopardi, Keith, *Sovereignty and the Stateless Nation: Gibraltar in the Modern Legal Context* (2009). Hart Publishing Ltd.

188 Gibraltar Chronicle (2001, 5th January)

189 EU Commission Press Release 11th July 2001 'Commission launches large scale state aid investigation' https://europa.eu/rapid/press-release_IP-01-982_en.htm (Last accessed on 26th February 2024)

The OECD blacklisting and the EU's State Aid investigation represented two major challenges for Gibraltar and marked the shifting international mood against previously-tolerated practices. There was mutual accord that a system which permitted the holding of undeclared and untaxed assets was not viable reputationally, and therefore compliance was necessary. Particularly in the context of its EU membership, Gibraltar could not stand alone when the norm was shifting away from financial services products based on no disclosure and no tax. Without going into the details and specifics of the State Aid investigation and the submissions proposed as part of this process, the end result was that, in the face of continued pressure, Gibraltar phased out the regimes which had attracted criticism. In terms of its status from an OECD perspective, Gibraltar's embrace of compliance culture during the 2000s saw it move from blacklist to greylist, and subsequently from greylist into whitelist, following the implementation of various tax information exchange agreements in line with OECD doctrine.

When it came to the OECD implementing its series of international 'Peer Reviews' in 2014, Gibraltar attained a favourable result and was ranked as a 'largely compliant' jurisdiction, alongside large economies such as UK, Germany and the USA. The OECD acknowledged that:

> 'Gibraltar has worked with the OECD in respect of tax information exchange since 2002 and since 2006 has participated in all of the Global Forum's annual assessments. In 2009 it became a member of the Global Forum and committed to the international standard for transparency and exchange of information for tax purposes. Since then it has quickly built up a network of exchange of information (EOI) agreement that includes its key trading partners.'[190]

This period also saw the introduction of the new Income Tax Act 2010 which sought definitively to resolve outstanding issues of uncertainty and the reputational damage inflicted by the EU's State Aid recommendations in 2005, and clearly

---

190 OECD 'Global Forum on Transparency and Exchange of Information for Tax Purposes Peer Reviews: Gibraltar 2014' (29th October 2014), available online on: https://read.oecd-ilibrary.org/taxation/global-forum-on-transparency-and-exchange-of-information-for-tax-purposes-peer-reviews-gibraltar-2014_9789264222885-en#page1 (Last accessed on 26th February 2024)

marked a departure from the 'offshore'" characteristics of the Exempt Company Regime which had been so criticised and a return to the base taxation system contained in the ITA 1952. The approach taken during this process demonstrates the desire (politically and more broadly within the private sector) to move towards a coherent tax framework, favouring excellence and quality over quantity and opaqueness.[191] The Government of Gibraltar's commitment to embracing the post-offshore world is epitomised in the following statement released during the new Income Tax Act consultation process:

> 'This legislation ends all distinction between "onshore" and "offshore" business. Together with the tax information exchange agreements being entered into by the Government, and Gibraltar's full integration in the EU and compliance with EU financial services regulation, money laundering and co-operation rules, the new Tax Act completes Gibraltar's 14 year transition from tax haven to mainstream European financial services centre.'[192]

The administration of Chief Minister Fabian Picardo, which took over from Caruana's government in 2011, has proceeded in a manner consistent with the continuing policy of embracing international norms and integrating the required obligations. It has complied with its obligations by making Gibraltar's tax system acceptable to the EU whilst remaining distinct from that of the UK, therefore protecting the autonomy, prosperity and continued self-sufficiency of the territory.

The International Obligations

This urge to enter into and comply with international regimes in order to embrace the post-1999 international taxation landscape that we have summarised above means that Gibraltar has regularly entered into and implemented international

191 Similar impulses can be seen in the approach taken by Gibraltar to gambling regulation, which emphasizes quality over quantity.

192 Government of Gibraltar Press Release No 150/2010 'Government Publishes New Draft Income Tax Act' 16 June 2010 retrieved from https://www.gibraltarlawyers.com/files/GovernmentpublishesnewdraftIncomeTaxActo.pdf (Last accessed on 26th February 2024)

regimes and amended its law in accordance with the requirements of the international community. It has attempted to be a leading jurisdiction amongst those of a similar nature in this area and this can be evidenced by the number of regimes it has entered into and complied with.

TIEAs – Tax Information Exchange Agreements

Tax Information Exchange Agreements ('TIEAs') provide a mechanism for the smooth transfer of tax information in order to assist the administration and enforcement of domestic tax laws. They are promoted by the OECD to develop and further international co-operation in tax matters. In effect, they are a mechanism adopted to avoid conflicts between jurisdictions on the access of information. Conflicts often emerge when, in order to enforce its own laws, a jurisdiction attempts to access information that may be protected under the legal system of another jurisdiction. These types of conflicts have generally been resolved through the execution of TIEAs.

The OECD has developed a model protocol which can be used by jurisdictions to facilitate the implementation of TIEAs and, accordingly, further their use globally. Gibraltar is able to negotiate its own TIEAs, which are then signed under Letters of Entrustment issued by the United Kingdom empowering Gibraltar to enter into such arrangements.

The first TIEA Gibraltar entered into was with the United States of America on 31st March 2009 (the 'US TIEA'). This resulted from a determination by the Internal Revenue Service of the United States of America that Gibraltar's know-your-customer rules are acceptable for the purposes of the Qualified Intermediary regime. As such, this facilitated reporting obligations for payments of income from the United States to an account holder through one or more foreign intermediaries.

This US TIEA has allowed access to information relevant to the administration and enforcement of the domestic laws of both countries concerning the taxes covered by the US TIEA.

Amendments to the US TIEA were incorporated in May 2014 via a protocol by adding a mechanism for automatic exchange of information and spontaneous exchange of information, thereby reinforcing Gibraltar's commitment to transparency and the furtherance of communication mechanisms with the United States.

To date, Gibraltar has entered in 27 TIEAs with a range of jurisdictions. These include 14 European Union Member States and other major countries around the world. The OECD and the Financial Action Task Force, members of which are the G-20 countries, have stated that a country must have a minimum of twelve TIEAs in order to be regarded as co-operating in matters of tax information exchange transparency. Given the size of its population, the quantity of TIEAs entered into by Gibraltar highlights the territory's continued commitment to transparency and co-operation in exchange of tax information. Further, it is widely understood that one of the key criteria in determining harmful tax practices is the effective exchange of information, at a system-wide level it is one of the factors identified by the OECD in its *Harmful Tax Competition: An Emerging Global Issue*[193] as a hallmark of a tax haven. Gibraltar's efforts in entering into a range of TIEAs have assisted the jurisdiction in improving its global image by demonstrating its foremost concern is its financial services offering.

In 2014 Gibraltar committed to the OECD and Council of Europe Multilateral Convention on Mutual Administrative Assistance in Tax Matters (the 'Convention'). The convention entered into force in Gibraltar by virtue of extension under Article 29 (territorial application). This Convention is widely regarded as the most comprehensive multilateral instrument available for all cooperation in tackling tax evasion and avoidance. This commitment has done away with the need for further bilateral TIEAs.

Mutual Convention on Mutual Administrative Assistance in Tax Matters

The Mutual Convention on Mutual Administrative Assistance in Tax Matters ('MCMAA') is an international convention developed by the OECD and the Council of Europe in 1988 (and subsequently amended by Protocol in 2010). It is branded by the OECD as 'the most comprehensive multilateral instrument available for all forms of tax-co-operation to tackle tax evasion and avoidance'.[194]

193 *Harmful Tax Competition: An Emerging Global Issue* [OECD] 1999 p22

194 Please see further: https://www.oecd.org/ctp/exchange-of-tax-information/convention-on-mutual-administrative-assistance-in-tax-matters.htm#:~:text=The%20Convention%20is%20the%20most,the%20fundamental%20rights%20of%20taxpayers

The convention entered into force with regard to Gibraltar on 1 March 2014 (through the extension by the United Kingdom of the MCMAA's territorial scope to cover Gibraltar). This follows the announcement from HM Government of Gibraltar in November 2013, indicating that Gibraltar Chief Minister Fabian Picardo had written to UK Prime Minister David Cameron requesting that the MCMAA be extended to Gibraltar. Providing further background to the rationale for this request, the announcement further declared that:

> 'Such an extension forms an integral part of the HM Government of Gibraltar's continuing policy of having Gibraltar recognised as being at the very forefront of jurisdictions seeking to eradicate tax evasion.'[195]

The MCMAA is implemented in Gibraltar via the Taxation (Mutual Administrative Assistance) Act 2014 (the 'MCMAA Act') and provides for tax information exchange and the recovery of foreign tax claims between Gibraltar and each of the countries and territories which have also ratified the MCMAA.[196] The MCMAA Act designates the Gibraltar Commissioner of Income Tax as the Competent Authority, whose principal functions include the exchange of information, participation in tax examinations abroad and liaising with relevant jurisdictions applying for administrative assistance in tax matters.

With regard to the basis upon which information on taxpayers may be exchanged between Gibraltar and other participating states, the MCMAA Act details that this will apply where such information is foreseeably relevant for the administration or enforcement of any laws, whether in Gibraltar or in the requesting state, which relate to taxes on income or profits. The scope of this is intended to be interpreted to the widest possible extent yet, simultaneously, to clarify that those requesting information cannot engage in 'fishing expeditions' or seek information that is unlikely to be relevant to the tax affairs of a given person or ascertainable group or category of persons.[197]

(Last accessed on 26th February 2024)

195 HM Government of Gibraltar Press Office, Press Release No 401/2013, 7th June 2013

196 To date this amounts to 147 jurisdictions (including all G20, BRIICS and OECD countries)

197 Council of Europe Explanatory Report to the Convention on Mutual Administrative Assistance in Tax Matters as amended by the 2010 Protocol, European Treaty Series –

IGA – Intergovernmental Agreements

FATCA

The USA's introduction of its Foreign Accounts Tax Compliance Act ('FATCA') imposed a reporting obligation on Financial Institutions (defined widely to include entities such as professionally-managed trusts and investment vehicles managed by other Financial Institutions) to declare all accounts or interests held by US persons to the US tax authorities, or otherwise suffer a withholding tax of 30% on US payments. For purposes of facilitating global FATCA compliance, the US Government began entering into Inter-governmental Agreements ('IGAs') with foreign governments under the Model 1 IGA in order to appoint a local competent authority to interact with the US authorities.[198]

In line with consistent Gibraltar Government policy (across various administrations since 2000) to engage with international tax compliance demands, Gibraltar and the USA signed an IGA called the 'Agreement between the Government of the United States of America and the Government of Gibraltar to Improve International Tax Compliance and to Implement FATCA' on 8th May 2014, and this entered into force on 17th September 2015[199] (but treated as being effective as from 30th June 2014). In accordance with its obligations under this IGA, Gibraltar legislation was amended on 19th August 2015 through the introduction of the International Co-operation (Improvement of International Tax Compliance) (United States) Regulations 2015. As demonstrated by the records kept by the US Treasury, Gibraltar formed part of the initial wave of territories to enter into and implement an IGA with the USA.[200]

No. 127, 01.VI.2011

198 There are several forms of IGA, Model 1A, 1B, 2A and 2B, each with a different approach to the interactions of the competent authorities and reciprocity.

199 The importance of the entry into force of this agreement between Gibraltar and the United States cannot be overestimated as a factor in the development of Gibraltar as a jurisdiction. It may well be the case that Peter Caruana (the then Chief Minister) was acting under Letters of Entrustment from the United Kingdom, but the sight of the Chief Minister of Gibraltar entering into an agreement with the Secretary of the Treasury of the United States in person had a significant psychological impact.

200 US Department of Treasury, Resource Centre, Foreign Account Tax Compliance Act available online: https://www.treasury.gov/resource-center/tax-policy/treaties/

UK FATCA

To cover the exchange of information on financial accounts in respect of the years 2014 to 2016 within the United Kingdom, its crown dependencies and overseas territories, the UK introduced its own, smaller, FATCA-like regime. Gibraltar and the UK agreed on its implementation on 21st November 2013, which in turn led to the enactment of the International Co-operation (Improvement of International Tax Compliance) (United Kingdom) Regulations 2015 in Gibraltar on 11th November 2015. This was a temporary measure given that, as set out later in this chapter, the UK and all the crown dependencies and overseas territories subsequently adopted the Common Reporting Standard ('CRS') which superseded the UK's FATCA-inspired regime. During the lifetime of the regime in Gibraltar, information was exchanged with the UK in full and on time.

Common Reporting Standards

Motivated by the USA's ambition under FATCA and following pressure and endorsements from prominent players on the international stage, the CRS framework for a global automatic information exchange system was proposed in the OECD's report titled 'A Step Change in Tax Transparency'[201] (the 'CRS Report') which aimed to utilise the model in the Model 1A IGA developed by the United States.

On 29th October 2014, Gibraltar implemented CRS by becoming a signatory to the OECD's Multilateral Competent Authority Agreement on the Automatic Exchange of Financial Account Information and through the entry into force of the International Co-operation (Improvement of International Tax Compliance) Regulations 2016 (the 'CRS Regs') on 22nd December 2016. Gibraltar's first exchange of information under the CRS system took place in September 2017, which was the earliest possible date.

It is interesting to note that Gibraltar implemented this system prior to several major jurisdictions, including Hong Kong, Israel and Japan. It is also worth noting that the United States elected not to participate at all.

Pages/FATCA.aspx (Last accessed on 26th February 2024)

201 Organisation for Economic Cooperation and Development 'A Step Change in Tax Transparency' June 2013 available online on: http://www.oecd.org/ctp/exchange-of-tax-information/taxtransparency_G8report.pdf (Last accessed on 26th February 2024)

The CRS Regs implemented 'Council Directive 2014/107/EU of 9th December 2014, and Council Directive (EU) 2015/2376 of 8 December 2015 both amending Directive 2011/16/EU as regards mandatory automatic exchange of information in the field of taxation', [202] thereby allowing Gibraltar to fulfil its obligations under EU law and the DAC.

The actions required to make the applicable changes to Gibraltar law were assumed by the Gibraltar Government with little to no discourse or consultation. It is curious to note that there was no debate in Gibraltar's Parliament surrounding the implementation of the CRS system, nor does Hansard record any objections on the part of the opposition to this state of affairs. Further, a review of the archives of the Gibraltar Chronicle and the Gibraltar Panorama produces no news reports or commentary relating to CRS implementation, other than mere factual reporting. This lack of comment is most likely to be driven by an acceptance that compliance and participation in the CRS is exactly the right course of action and that Gibraltar should be a responsible member of the international community of tax jurisdictions. Whilst increasing the administrative burden on the finance centre, the behaviour of the Gibraltar Government and the wider community demonstrates that non-compliance was not considered as an option.

EU Directives

The United Kingdom joined the European Economic Community on 1 January 1973, via the Treaty of Accession 1972. Gibraltar joined alongside the United Kingdom via the European Communities Act 1972 as a dependant territory of the United Kingdom. Subsequently EU law applied in Gibraltar, pursuant to Article 355(3) of the Treaty on the Functioning of the European Union (the 'EU Treaty') which provides that 'European territories for whose external relations a Member State is responsible'. Therefore, although Gibraltar did not itself form part of the United Kingdom, the United Kingdom remained responsible for Gibraltar's external relations.

202 Preamble to the CRS Regs., available online on: https://www.gibraltarlaws.gov.gi/uploads/legislations/taxation-mutual-administrative-assistance/2016s253/2016s253(10-07-20).pdf#viewer.action=download (Last accessed on 26th February 2024)

Accordingly, between 1972 and 2020, EU law applied in Gibraltar,[203] subject to a few exemptions, such as the European Union Customs Union, the Common Agricultural Policy, commercial policy provisions and Schengen Area (given the United Kingdon opted out of the Schengen Agreement).

EU law was given effect locally via the Gibraltar Communities Act 1972. His Majesty's Government of Gibraltar and the Gibraltar Parliament were responsible for the transposition and implementation of all European Union measures. During its membership, Gibraltar transposed legislative acts to implement and meet the goals of the European Union Directives.

The Gibraltar Income Tax Act 2010 currently transposes 13 different EU directives including:

1. Council Directive 2011/16/EU of 15 February 2011 on administrative cooperation in the field of taxation and repealing Directive 77/799/EEC and its amending Directives 2011/16/EU as regards mandatory automatic exchange of information in the field of taxation; (EU) 2016/881 as regards mandatory automatic exchange of information in the field of taxation; and (EU) 2016/2258 as regards access to anti-money-laundering information by tax authorities.
2. Council Directive 2011/96/EU of 30 November 2011 on the common system of taxation applicable in the case of parent companies and subsidiaries of different Member States and its amending Directives 2014/86/EU on the common system of taxation applicable in the case of parent companies and subsidiaries of different Member States and (EU) 2015/121 on the common system of taxation applicable in the case of parent companies and subsidiaries of different Member States;
3. Council Directive (EU) 2016/1164 of 12 July 2016 laying down rules against tax avoidance practices that directly affect the functioning of the internal market (ATAD II);
4. Council Directive (EU) 2017/952 of 29 May 2017 amending Directive (EU) 2016/1164 as regards hybrid mismatches with third countries, which is explained in further detail below;
5. Council Directive (EU) 2018/822 of 25 May 2018 amending Directive 2011/16/EU as regards mandatory automatic exchange of information in

203 Since 2020 Gibraltar has opted to retain much EU Law.

> the field of taxation in relation to reportable cross-border arrangements. Following Brexit, on 21st January 2021 HM Government of Gibraltar published a notice in the Gibraltar Gazette[204] to enact secondary legislation called the Income Tax Act 2010 (Amendment) (EU Exit) Regulations 2021 to extend the territorial application of this Directive, by realigning its reporting requirements under the retained provisions of this Directive to the standard required by the Organisation for Economic Co-operation and Development.

Many of these will be discussed by our fellow author Isaac Endfield in Chapter 7, particularly the provisions of ATAD II which implemented rules on interest limitation, hybrid mismatches, controlled foreign companies, an exit tax and mandated a general anti-avoidance rule. We do not propose to review them here, save to note that they are implemented and will be maintained.

His Majesty's Government of Gibraltar has publicly committed to maintain the existing EU Directives which have been transposed into Gibraltar law and, further, to consider whether the provisions of future Directives should be replicated in Gibraltar law. As a result, Gibraltar's offering will remain aligned with its competitors within the European Union.

DAC6 and the OECD Mandatory Disclosure Rules

Prior to January 2021, Gibraltar had enacted a mandatory disclosure regime based on the Council Directive (EU) 2018/822 ('DAC6') which introduced requirements on intermediaries (such as tax advisors, lawyers and accountants) to report on individuals involved in cross-border arrangements where certain hallmarks apply.

The United Kingdom had also previously adhered to the DAC6 framework. However, in what has been described as 'one of the first manifestations of the UK's new legislative freedom following the end of the EU exit transition period on 31 December 2020',[205] the free trade agreement entered into between the UK

---

204 Gibraltar Gazette Legal Notice No. 78 of 2021 dated Thursday 21st January 2021.

205 STEP Industry News (7th January 2021) – UK withdraws from most of DAC6's disclosure provisions UK withdraws from most of DAC6's disclosure provisions | STEP,

and the EU committed the parties to compliance with the OECD standards on mandatory disclosure, but did not require either party to go beyond them. Gibraltar, which also left the EU alongside the UK as part of Brexit, subsequently followed the path set by the UK on mandatory disclosure rules, by withdrawing from the DAC6 regime and aligning its reporting requirements with the OECD mandatory disclosure rules.

Gibraltar implemented these changes by enacting the Income Tax Act 2010 (Amendment) (EU Exit) Regulations 2021 which replicate the corresponding UK statutory position and are deemed to have come into effect as of 1st January 2021. Trimming away many of the elements of the DAC6 regime, the new approach compels reporting of arrangements only in cases intended to undermine reporting of financial accounts under the CRS, or cases relating to an arrangement involving a 'non-transparent legal or beneficial ownership chain'.

The Code of Conduct Group

The EU Code of Conduct Group was first established in 1998 to primarily assess tax measures that may fall within their scope with a focus on harmful tax practices. Although not binding, Member States agreed to roll back existing tax measures that were not in line with the Code and refrain from introducing any new harmful tax practices. Gibraltar has fully adopted this approach.

The EU Code of Conduct Group have, in the past, reviewed the Gibraltar Income Tax Act. In 2013 their review found the Act to be compliant with EU laws in all areas with the exception of the non-taxation of interest receivable arising on inter-group transactions. Following this finding and the EU Commission state aid investigation into limited aspects of the corporate tax regime in Gibraltar an amendment was made to the Act which resulted in a new tax, at the corporate tax rate (now 12.5%), being introduced on interest received or receivable by a Gibraltar company arising from an inter-company loan with an exemption where the interest received, or receivable is less than £100,000 per annum.

Following this change His Majesty's Government of Gibraltar made representations to the Code Group on 29 May 2013. These were favourably considered and the Code Group voted in Gibraltar's favour and endorsed

accessed 20th June 2023

Gibraltar's Income Tax Act as being complaint with the EU Code of Conduct Business Taxation. In his Ministerial Statement to Parliament, the Chief Minister Fabian Picardo stated, 'Gibraltar can and will adhere to EU and international standards and will prosper in the process of doing so'.[206]

In 2017 the EU Council established the EU list of non-cooperative jurisdictions for tax purposes. There are a host of measures which must be met to ensure compliance and be considered a cooperative jurisdiction.

The measures relate to tax transparency, fair taxation and measures against base erosion and profit shifting which are often referred to as 'anti-BEPS measures'. In summary it requires, amongst other matters, the jurisdictions to have implemented the Common Reporting Standards and to be largely compliant with the global forum on automatic exchange of information; that the jurisdiction should have no preferential tax measures that could be regarded as harmful by the Code of Conduct Group and finally, the implementation of 'anti-BEPS measures'. The measurement of this element via this mechanism has been adopted by the EU to ensure compliance with these measures, as failure to do so will result in the jurisdiction being added to the list of non-cooperative jurisdictions for tax purposes.

Gibraltar remains engaged on these measures and will look to keep up this standard as the measures develop, to ensure compliance, and avoid being added to the EU list of non-cooperative jurisdictions.

Base Erosion Profit Shifting and the OECD Inclusive Framework

The Base Erosion and Profit Shifting ('BEPS') project has been undertaken by the OECD to eliminate the erosion of participants' tax bases by the shifting of profits out of the jurisdictions which would otherwise benefit from tax collection.

The initial output of BEPS was a list of 15 action points presented to the OECD for approval in 2013, each action point was then fleshed out with a number of recommendations. As an EU jurisdiction during the period 2013 – 2020, Gibraltar was obliged to implement all the Directives which were issued to implement the BEPS action points. This gave rise to a number of the provisions which have been highlighted here and discussed in detail elsewhere in this work.

206 HM Government of Gibraltar Press Release No. 441/2013 dated 24th June 2013

One of the main criticisms of the OECD BEPS project is that it is a creature of the members of the OECD rather than a broad base of international jurisdictions. This is certainly true of the early parts of the project such as the BEPS Action Points. However, since the inauguration of the Inclusive Framework in 2016 there has been an attempt to expand the negotiating base.[207] Prior to 2019 Gibraltar had been excluded from the Inclusive Framework due to the objections of the Spanish authorities. However, partly as a result of the conclusion of a tax treaty between the UK and Spain regarding Gibraltar,[208] that objection was withdrawn. As Chief Minister Fabian Picardo said at the time;

> Our joining the OECD BEPS framework as a full and equal member is another demonstration of Gibraltar's commitment to international standards of tax transparency and cooperation. It is also a tangible deliverable resulting from the conclusion of the International Tax Treaty with Spain.[209]

Here we can see Gibraltar taking all the steps it can to participate. It is not a member of the UN, nor was it a member state of the EU, but by entering the Inclusive Framework it has signalled not only that it will implement all that which it is obliged to implement, but also that it will participate at any level at which it is permitted to in the formulation of a global policy.

The most obvious consequence of this participation in the Inclusive Framework was the agreement of the members of the Inclusive Framework to the terms of the 'Statement on a Two-Pillar Solution to Address the Tax Challenges Arising from the Digitalisation of the Economy' on 8th October 2021. This agreement proposed the implementation for a two-pillar proposal to radically overhaul the international taxation system in connection with multi-national enterprises. The Two-Pillar Solution is the most important revision of that system for 100 years.

---

207 Despite this there remain many criticisms of the OECD Inclusive Framework in terms of agenda setting and procedure. For a comprehensive summary of the issues see de la Feria, R., The Perceived (Un)Fairness of the Global Minimum Corporate Tax Rate (August 31, 2022). In W. Haslehner et al (eds), The Pillar 2 Global Minimum Tax (Edward Elgar, 2023), forthcoming, Available at SSRN: https://ssrn.com/abstract=4205720 (Last accessed on 26th February 2024)

208 For an extensive discussion of this treaty, see Chapter 8.

209 HM Government of Gibraltar Press Release 521/2019

This chapter is not the place to discuss the content of the Two-Pillar Solution. Much ink has already been spilt on that topic before a single penny of tax has been levied under it. However, it is relevant to our thesis that the only mandatory action required of any of the signatories of the 8th October statement is that, whilst they are not required to implement the rules to be developed, they will take no steps to interfere with the implementation of such rules by others. Thus, all that is required of Gibraltar is that it does nothing.

Instead of taking this passive role, Chief Minister Fabian Picardo went further than the minimum requirements when he confirmed in his 2023 budget speech that:

> 'In summing up on Pillar 2, Mr Speaker, I would like to reiterate the government's commitment to implementing a domestic regime that meets the objectives of the Pillar 2 initiative whilst maintaining economic prosperity for both our business community and the jurisdiction at large.'

Here we can see the fundamental policy of all governments in Gibraltar since the turn of the century. This is one, not only of compliance but also of active participation in the international community of taxing jurisdictions, whilst holding onto the economic interests of the jurisdiction.

Conclusion

As set out within this chapter, the actions of recent governments in Gibraltar demonstrate its proactive approach to compliance and transparency, especially in the context of maintaining a reputable financial centre and its post-colonial vision. There is clearly political will on all sides to remain a fully compliant participant and to continue meeting and implementing international obligations.

It is acknowledged by all that Gibraltar needs to be a modern and fiscally responsible participant in the international community of tax jurisdictions. It participates in the Inclusive Framework of the OECD and has undertaken to implement the GloBE Digitalisation of the Economy Pillar 2 Rules by 2025. There are no further steps that Gibraltar can take to implement international regimes that are recommended by the international community for a compliant jurisdiction. It is unlikely that this policy perspective will change in the foreseeable future.

Chapter 6

COMPLIANCE, COMPLIANCE, COMPLIANCE

The Principle of the Enforcement of Compliance

Isaac Endfield

Introduction

In its simplest form, anti-avoidance legislation is legislation that tackles the avoidance of tax. A range of factors have brought the subject of 'tax avoidance' firmly into the public sphere, these include the 07/08 financial crisis, along with major tax scandals over prior decades, large corporations funnelling their profits into tax-free jurisdictions through, for example, IP schemes, and governments offering significant tax incentives to entities willing to invest in their jurisdictions. Consequently, the Organisation for Economic Cooperation and Development ('OECD') — an inter-governmental organisation consisting of the world's major economies — and the G20 — an inter-governmental forum consisting of 19 countries and the EU — began to focus on the issue. The OECD and G20 then joined forces, commencing work on the Base Erosion & Profit Shifting Project. This was a successful enterprise, still bearing fruit in the form of guidance and draft legal texts today, with the sole aim of tackling tax avoidance, improving transparency in the market, and creating a unanimous anti-tax-avoidance harmonisation strategy.

Wishing to take the lead on confronting tax avoidance, the European Union then took up these draft legal instruments and transformed them into anti-avoidance laws including AEOI, CbCR, ATADs 1 & 2, and the Directive on Administrative Cooperation version 6 (amongst others). The ATAD 1 Directive introduced the General Anti-Avoidance Rules (GAARs) which imposed upon all EU Member States an obligation to introduce the General Anti-Avoidance Rules into their domestic legislation, and also introduced the Specific Anti-Avoidance Rules (SAARs). ATAD 2 is an updated ATAD 1, which incorporated additional Hybrid Mismatches. Interestingly, a couple of decades before this, the 'new realism' approach to tax avoidance had begun to gain momentum in the United Kingdom, where the English case of *Ramsay v IRC*[210] had seen the House of Lords strike down a convoluted tax avoidance scheme by looking at the substance of the transactions as a whole, rather than focusing on each individual strictly legal step. Fast forward to 2001, Lord Hoffman's well-known dissent in *Westmoreland v MacNiven*[211] brought about, in the UK, at least, discussions in Parliament about implementing a general anti-avoidance law into statute.

Having provided a brief background, the chapter will now move on to discuss the anti-avoidance project and the principle of enforcement of compliance from a Gibraltar perspective. This chapter will demonstrate that for well over 110 years, Gibraltar has had, and has, a rich and deep history of tackling tax avoidance and has embraced the anti-avoidance legislative frameworks introduced by the Base Erosion Profit Shifting Project (BEPS). This chapter will first review Mr Peter Caruana's speech in the Gibraltar Parliament on the 'Climate of Compliance' as a background to the change in Gibraltar. Following that, there will be a brief introduction to general and specific anti-avoidance measures, after which, this chapter will review the broader developments of the GAAR, before moving on to review the Gibraltar GAAR in greater detail. Prior to its conclusion, the chapter will then review the SAARs from a Gibraltar perspective.

Gibraltar - Historical Background

Gibraltar's Climate of Compliance

In the Second Reading of the 2010 Income Tax Bill (the 'Bill')[212] — which became the Gibraltar Income Tax Act 2010 — the former Chief Minister of Gibraltar, Mr Peter Caruana said that 'this Bill, if passed by the House... will bring our tax system closer into the mainstream of conventional tax systems and make Gibraltar's corporate tax regime less exceptional than it has been in the past. More acceptable to the international community, less of the sort required by more brass-plate, tax-haven-type finance centre jurisdictions and more in keeping with the more mainstream onshore-type European financial services jurisdictions that Gibraltar

210 *W T Ramsay v IRC* (1979) 54 TC 101

211 *Westmoreland Investments Limited v MacNiven HL* [2001] STC 237

212 This subsequently became the Income Tax Act 2010.

has carefully tried to reposition itself towards in the last dozen years or so.'[213]

Caruana expressed that the Government of Gibraltar aimed to make the Bill and eventual new legislation 'as compliant as possible with known emerging international consensuses, such as OECD and EU Code of Conduct'.[214] Furthermore, Caruana explained in his speech that if Gibraltar was going to adopt a more competitive corporate tax rate of 10%, then a firmer attitude towards compliance and enforcement would be required.[215] The Government of Gibraltar dubbed this strategy a 'climate of compliance', which is not just about 'protecting revenue in a context of lower rates, [but] also... expecting people who get the benefit of lower rates to at least be more compliant'.[216] Caruana further pointed out that tightening up the enforcement regime provided fairness to the obedient taxpayers: 'making people who do not pay, pay what they should... increases Government revenue, which the Government can then apply to reducing the tax bill for everybody else as well.'[217]

Caruana went on to explain that the 'significant and comprehensive anti-avoidance measures are introduced to prevent the escape by legal means.'[218] The thinking behind this, mentioned in the speech, is that the difference between the lower rate corporation taxation and the higher level of personal taxation created the perfect conditions for people to integrate personal tax liability into a corporate tax burden.[219] In an effort to expand on the climate of compliance, Caruana then listed the six steps integral to its creation, from altering the date of tax due, to tightening penalties for false returns, to the 'Name and Shame' list. This led smoothly on to the topic of effective avoidance, with Caruana conveying that the Bill 'refers to anti-avoidance provisions to ensure that the system is as resilient as possible to being planned around, and also to ensure that if anybody comes up with a clever idea for getting around the system... the Government and Parliament

---

213 Hansard 20th October 2010 page 27, para 1, Hansard 2010 (parliament.gi), accessed 5th July 2023

214 Ibid, para 2.

215 Ibid page 28, para 2.

216 Ibid.

217 Ibid.

218 Ibid, para 3.

219 Hansard 20th October 2010 page 28, para 1, Hansard 2010 (parliament.gi), accessed 5th July 2023

can get to hear of it as quickly as possible and decide whether it wants to close the loopholes.'[220]

Prior to this, the anti-avoidance measures in the Income Tax Act 1952 (the previous taxation act in Gibraltar), were very much based on the belief that taxpayers were content with paying taxes as due. However, Caruana pointed out, 'as the tax paying populations become more sophisticated at organising their affairs in relation to their tax liabilities... so too the tax system has to keep up with these developments and protect itself from increasingly cleverer and far-reaching means of circumventing its requirements.'[221] The Bill introduced three routes to keep up to date with such developments: (i) general anti-avoidance clauses; (ii) specific anti-avoidance clauses; and (iii) the notification regime.

The following paragraphs will provide a basic overview of these three strategies, taking each in order, before they are explored later in the chapter, from both international and local perspectives.

Generic & Specific Anti-Avoidance

General Anti-Avoidance

The general anti-avoidance rules ('GAARs') are a set of measures, acting as a last remedy, which permit a government under the guidance of its tax authority to pass laws that prohibit avoidance strategies that would have otherwise complied with the regular statutory understanding of the existing tax law legislation. As Waerzeggers explains, 'a GAAR is typically designed to strike down those otherwise lawful practices that are found to be carried out in a manner which undermines the intention of the tax law such as where a taxpayer has misused or abused that law. This is typically achieved by giving the authority the power to cancel a particular tax benefit or asses a different [normally increased] tax liability against the taxpayer in circumstances where the course of action taken by a taxpayer is so blatant, artificial, or contrived that it is only explicable by the desire to obtain a relevant tax benefit.'[222] Stewart points out that modern GAARs 'emphasise the

---

220 Ibid.

221 Hansard 20th October 2010 page 38, para 1, Hansard 2010 (parliament.gi), accessed 5th July 2023

222 Christophe Waerzeggers and Cory Hillier, 'Introducing a General Anti-Avoidance

objective facts and taxpayer purpose, and focus on the economic or commercial substance of a transaction as opposed to its legal form'.[223]

Specific Anti-Avoidance

The specific anti-avoidance rules ('SAARs') are a set of rules — including the thin-capitalisation rule, transactions with connected persons, transfer of assets abroad regime, the interest limitation rule, exit tax regime, controlled foreign company rules and the hybrid mismatch rules — all of which aim to combat known tax avoidance arrangements.

Notification Regime

This is a regime which provides for advance tax rulings. This regime is similar to the UK's DOTAS, but in a simplified form. Essentially, it seeks to promote clarity in regard to the execution of tax legislature for the authority and taxpayer. Most countries have a notification regime of some sort.

GAARs in the International Context

The next couple of paragraphs will explore the general development of the GAAR with a focus on its implementation in Australia, China, the Netherlands, the UK and in the EU.

The Broader Development of GAARs

GAARs continue to develop worldwide to create tax systems which are avoidance-free. While GAARs differ country-to-country, most countries have adopted somewhat similar codes to empower their tax authorities, with the ability to strike down taxpayers' arrangements to gain tax benefits at their core. GAARs are not a new idea. New Zealand's is understood to be well over a hundred-and-thirty

Rule' (GAAR) [2016] 1(01) Tax Law IMF Technical Note 3

223 Miranda Stewart, *Tax and Government in the 21st Century* (1st edn, Cambridge University Press 2022) 248

years old.[224] Similarly, Australia has had a GAAR in its income tax legislation since its inauguration in 1915, with the 'first federal GAAR in s 53 of the Income Tax Act 1915, referring to tax avoidance in the older judicial language of "sham and evasion"'.[225] In Australia, three principles must be found for the tax authorities to have the power to issue a revised income tax assessment. Firstly, a scheme must be identified. Secondly, the scheme must give rise to a tax benefit for a taxpayer. Thirdly, the sole or dominant purpose of one or more parties to the scheme is to obtain that tax benefit for that taxpayer.[226]

This can be contrasted with China's GAAR, which was introduced in 2008 by the Chinese Corporate Income Tax Law 2008. Under this regime, the tax authorities 'have the right to adjust and impose tax on arrangements entered into by an enterprise that is without reasonable commercial purpose and that results in an elimination, reduction or deferral of taxable income'.[227] In the Netherlands, the legal doctrine of 'fraus legis' or abuse of law exceeded the 1987 statutory GAAR 'as it applies to all forms of taxation and not just direct taxes and enables transactions to be disregarded or recharacterised in appropriate circumstances'.[228] The doctrine requires: firstly, that the tax avoidance was 'the sole or prevailing motive of the taxpayer in entering into a particular set of interrelated legal actions and factual operations (the 'arrangement'); and, secondly, that the fiscal outcome of the arrangement is contrary to the object and purpose of the provisions of the tax law concerned'.[229]

The above implementations differ from the UK GAAR, which is not composed like the fraus legis doctrine and is not a broad-spectrum rule. Rather, the UK GAAR is 'intended to deter taxpayers from entering into the most abusive and contrived schemes, while leaving the clear centre ground of tax planning

224 C. Ellife, 'New Zealand's General Anti-Avoidance Rule – A Triumph of Flexibility Over Certainty' (2014) 62 Canadian Tax Journal 147.

225 from KIDS plain v4.0 (austlii.edu.au)

226 PWC, 'General Anti-Avoidance Rules' (PWC's Recent Global Developments, 14 October 2016) available online on: https://www.pwc.com/gx/en/tax/newsletters/tax-controversy-dispute-resolution/assets/pwc-TCDR%20Insights-GAAR-recent-developments.pdf (last accessed on 26th February 2024)

227 Ibid.

228 Ibid.

229 Ibid.

undisturbed.'[230] In this regard, the GAAR is trigged by 'tax arrangements' that are 'abusive'. Roughly, a 'tax arrangement' is an arrangement 'which, viewed objectively, has the obtaining of a tax advantage as its main purpose or purposes.'[231] An arrangement will be 'abusive' where HMRC can show that it cannot 'reasonably be regarded as a reasonable course of action.'[232] For this, the 'double reasonableness test' is deployed, which asks 'would a reasonable person hold the view that the arrangement was a reasonable course of action?'[233]

Focusing back on the EU, by 2002 'only a few EU Member States had neither a GAAP, nor a GAAR, in their legal systems and those that did not, have approved one since, either independently or as a result of EU jurisprudence and legislation.'[234] In 2016, the European Commission ('EC') introduced Anti-Tax Avoidance Directive I ('ATAD').[235] ATAD 1 introduced a package of reforms which target aggressive tax planning and increase transparency. One of the six reforms includes Article 6, which introduced the EU GAAR across the EU.

ATAD I, Article 6 provides:

1. For the purposes of calculating the corporate tax liability, a Member State shall ignore an arrangement or a series of arrangements which, having been put into place for the main purpose or one of the main purposes of obtaining a tax advantage that defeats the object or purpose of the applicable tax law, are not genuine having regard to all relevant facts and circumstances. An arrangement may comprise more than one step or part.
2. For the purposes of paragraph 1, an arrangement or a series thereof shall be regarded as non-genuine to the extent that they are not put into place for valid commercial reasons which reflect economic reality.
3. Where arrangements or a series thereof are ignored in accordance with

230 Ibid.

231 HMRC, HMRC's GAAR Guidance (2013) 9

232 HMRC, HMRC's GAAR Guidance (2013) 10

233 HMRC, HMRC's GAAR Guidance (2013) 10

234 Rita Glen Loutzenhiser and Rita de la Feria, *The Dynamics of Taxation - Essays in Honour of Judith Freedman* (1st edn, Hart Publishing 2020) 176

235 European Commission, 'Proposal for a Council Directive laying down rules against tax avoidance

practices that directly affect the functioning of the internal market' COM(2016) 26 final.

> paragraph 1, the tax liability shall be calculated in accordance with national law.

ATAD 1 clearly provides an instruction for all Member States to introduce a measure to strike down arrangements which have been put into place for the main purpose of obtaining a tax advantage which defeats the object or purpose of the applicable law.

For such wide matters to be implemented across all EU Member States, there must be unanimity by ECOFIN,[236] which interestingly was the case with the EU GAAR. De La Feria expresses that 'although EU harmonisation within direct taxation has traditionally been slow, with proposals lingering for years on the EU policy agenda, the ATAD was adopted merely six months after it was proposed'.[237] Furthermore, Feria argues that the speed at which the proposal was adopted 'is undoubtedly symptomatic of the trend towards, and political momentum behind the introduction of a new, general anti-tax mechanism, but it is also indicative of how little scrutiny its provisions were subject to'.[238] Delle also raises concerns over the speed at which the EU GAAR was adopted, alongside questioning the level of scrutiny it undertook, which was lacking in comprehensive technical discussions and impact assessments.[239] That said, the adopted form of any GAAR must cater to each jurisdiction's respective legal systems and nuances, and therefore varies from member state to member state.

The Danger of GAARs and the Large Amount of Discretion

The introduction of GAARs is not without concerns. Due to its form, the GAAR is not the business of the taxpayer, rather the determination must be made by the respective tax authority through an assessment process. Waerzeggers argues that the stated objective of stamping out unacceptable tax avoidance makes the drafting of a GAAR highly complex, as 'the phrase "tax avoidance" means different things

236 Economics and Financial Affairs Council

237 Rita Glen Loutzenhiser and Rita de la Feria, *The Dynamics of Taxation - Essays in Honour of Judith Freedman* (1st edn, Hart Publishing 2020) 179

238 Ibid.

239 A. C. Delle, 'The EU Anti-Avoidance Directive: a UK Perspective' [2016] BTR 490

to different people'.[240] While the drafted GAAR should strike down artificial arrangements which are tax motivated, the GAAR 'should be designed and applied so as to not inhibit or impede ordinary commercial transactions in respect of which taxpayers can legitimately take advantage of opportunities available to them when structuring or carrying out those transactions'.[241]

Furthermore, the ability of tax authorities to distinguish between tax arrangements that fall within or outside of the GAAR will involve a highly delicate analysis, and of necessity an amount of discretion. In a similar light, Hellier argues that 'the success of a GAAR in achieving its purpose will ultimately depend on (1) the legal design and drafting of the GAAR, and (2) the capacity of the tax authority appropriately to apply the GAAR in a measured, even handed and predictable way'.[242]

David Goldberg KC vocalised his concern about the GAAR and pronounced it as 'an affront to the rule of law: a provision which we should be ashamed to have enacted'.[243] Goldberg KC concedes that this statement comes from a mix of rational and emotional thoughts. However, he argues, this is because 'a GAAR deals with a subject which brings forth an intensely emotional response to the question, "Is this abusive tax avoidance?"'[244] Therefore, Goldberg KC argues that the GAAR 'not only permits but encourages and requires an enquiry of the emotions and elevates out response into law".[245] He posits that 'to the observer who says "I don't like what the taxpayer has done", the problem seems to be one of taxpayer behaviour, which needs to be swatted like an irritating fly'.[246] In response to that, Goldberg KC argues that the 'very purpose of the tax legislation is to set reasonably defined boundaries: it is to say here there is tax, there is none; here

240 Christophe Waerzeggers and Cory Hillier, 'Introducing a General Anti-Avoidance Rule' (GAAR) [2016] 1(01) Tax Law IMF Technical Note 3

241 Ibid.

242 Christophe Waerzeggers and Cory Hillier, 'Introducing a General Anti-Avoidance Rule' (GAAR) [2016] 1(01) Tax Law IMF Technical Note 3

243 David Goldberg KC, 'Reflections on the GAAR' [2021] Vol XII No.2 'GITC Review' 26

244 Ibid

245 Ibid

246 David Goldberg KC, 'Reflections on the GAAR' [2021] Vol XII No.2 'GITC Review' 27

there is relief, there not... the chief function of a detailed tax code is to allow the taxpayer to do things which are outside the tax net: and we should all prefer that system to those in force in Tudor times, when there was much more discretion given to the tax gatherer than has, in recent times, been commonly usual'.[247] In line with Goldberg KC's argument, not only does a general catch-all clause make actions outside the tax net so much more confusing; but it worsens the lack of a sense present in the tax code. Goldberg KC concludes that the 'spirit of the law is like the wind: it cannot read, and it cannot be read; it certainly cannot be read when the code in question does not have a coherent common thread running through it, and the addition of the GAAR... is more likely to increase fraud than it is likely to improve tax collection'.[248]

Prebble and Prebble point out that the GAAR is necessary because there are 'situations where the legislator will want to close a loophole that has not been defined in advance. Principally, if the legislators could foresee all varieties of tax avoidance, they would pass specifically targeted rules to frustrate those endeavours. No doubt, most tax policy makers could give examples of the sorts of arrangements that might be caught by general anti-avoidance rules, but these examples would be cases that have been found to constitute avoidance in the past. The fact that GAARs exist at all is evidence that policy-makers and legislators themselves cannot predict what structures taxpayers will eventually contrive'.[249]

The author respectfully disagrees with Prebble and other like-minded, academic approaches. The point of a tax system, certainly the larger and more detailed it becomes, is to provide a clearer and more defined framework. Yes, one can deduct this here; no, one cannot here; this forms part of your tax base; this does not. First, it is up to the legislator to specify exactly what taxes will be levied on the taxpayer, and not for them to produce a colander through which all commercial arrangements are drained. There is always a give and take between the taxpayer and the authority; a yin and yang. In the author's opinion, with the implementation

247 David Goldberg KC, 'Reflections on the GAAR' [2021] Vol XII No.2 'GITC Review' 28

248 David Goldberg KC, 'Reflections on the GAAR' [2021] Vol XII No.2 'GITC Review' 33

249 Rebecca Prebble and John Prebble, 'Does the use of GAARs to combat tax avoidance breach principles of the rule of law', [2012] 2 (02) Victoria University of Wellington Legal Research Papers 29-30

of the GAAR, certainly in the UK, the pendulum may have swung too far in the favour of the tax authority. For example, in the UK, the tax codes amount to over 80,000 pages and yet nowhere do they explain what taxpayers can and cannot do. Finally, on top of the existing onerous obligations, the tax authority introduces a catch-all test; that is to say, whatever transaction or arrangement is entered into, the authorities will subject it to an over-arching, one-size-fits-all assessment. There may be a degree of subjectivity concerning the artificiality or fictitiousness of arrangement X or transaction Y, but should the case go before the judiciary, the results may be skewed to an extent by the very subjectivity that those 80,000+ pages of tax code were drafted to prevent.

The Gibraltar GAAR

Historical Gibraltar Background and the Proto GAAR

The general background on GAARs leads us neatly to the Gibraltar GAAR. It can be argued that the Gibraltar GAAR is another feather in the cap for the territory, in terms of its firm and long-standing approach to anti-avoidance. In fact, Gibraltar has had two forms of a general anti-avoidance mechanism, potentially a proto GAAR, since 1922, stemming from the Model Income Tax Ordinance from the Report of the Inter-Departmental Committee on Income Tax (the 'Model Ordinance 1922')[250] and incorporated into the Income Tax Act 1952 ('ITA 1952') and the second hiding away in ITA 1952.

The Model Ordinance 1922, s 40 provided:

> 'Where it appears to the Commissioner that any person liable to additional tax has not been assessed or has been assessed at a less amount than that assessments, which ought to have been charged, the Commissioner may, within the year of assessment or within two years after the expiration thereof, assess such person at such amount or additional amount, as according to his judgment ought to have been charged, and the provisions of this Ordinance as to notice of assessment, appeal and other proceedings under this Ordinance shall apply to such assessment or additional assessment and to the tax charged

250 Report on the Inter-Departmental Committee on Income Tax in the Colonies not Possessing Responsible Government - the Model Income Tax Ordinance 1922

thereunder.'

Section 40 provided the Income Tax Commissioner with the ability to reassess a person's tax liability at such amount as ought to have been charged according to his judgement (my emphasis). This general anti-avoidance article — albeit expanded to include no deadline to re-assess in cases where fraud and wilful default was committed — was incorporated verbatim in the Gibraltar ITA 1952 at s 74.[251]

Additionally, the ITA 1952, s 13(1) provided an alternative proto GAAR:

> 'Where the Commissioner is of the opinion that any transaction which reduces or would reduce the amount of tax payable by any person is artificial or fictitious or that any disposition is not in fact given effect to, he may disregard any such transaction or disposition and the persons concerned shall be assessable accordingly.'

According to Caruana, ITA 2010, s 40 (which will be discussed below) 'restates section 13 [above] in a way, which strengthens the intent of the previous Act (ITA 52) and allows the Minister to make regulation to give effect to that intent [through the introduction of ITA 2010, s 40(2)]'.[252] Section 40, in other words, provides the Minister a 'general regulatory making power to enable regulations to be passed quickly to close avoidance mechanisms that are discovered'.[253]

The Modern Day Gibraltar GAAR

ITA 2010, s 40 not only provides a stronger intent and general regulation-making powers, but also incorporates Schedule 4, which contains the Specific Anti-Avoidance Rules ('SAARs'), to be explored later in the chapter.

ITA 2010, s 40 incorporates the modern-day Gibraltar GAAR:

---

251 Income Tax Act 1952 (although cited as Income Tax Act), section 74

252 Hansard 20th October 2010 page 38, para 1, Hansard 2010 (parliament.gi), accessed 5th July 2023

253 Ibid.

(1.) 'Where the Commissioner believes that a person who is or would otherwise be chargeable to taxation in accordance with this Act has entered into an arrangement which eliminates, reduces or would eliminate or reduce the amount of the taxation payable and that arrangement is artificial, is fictitious or has elements which are artificial or fictitious, he may disregard the arrangement or those parts of it which eliminate or reduce the taxation payable and assess the person on the amount of the taxation due in the absence of the arrangement or those parts of the arrangement which the Commissioner disregards.

(2.) The Minister may make regulations for the purposes of preventing the avoidance of liability to tax by any fictitious or artificial arrangements or any other arrangements which have as their aim or effect the elimination or reduction of tax which would otherwise be due or payable.

(3.) This section shall be construed in such manner as best secures consistency between:
   a. subsection (1) above;
   b. internationally accepted principles for the determination of profit in respect of activities within a multinational group of companies, notably the rules which, at the date this Act came into effect, were contained in Article 9 of the Model Tax Convention on Income and on Capital published by the OECD;
   c. all the documents published by the OECD, at any time before the date this Act came into effect, as part of their Transfer Pricing Guidelines for Multinational Enterprises and Tax Administrations, together with such documents issued by that Organisation on or after the date this Act came into effect which are designated by an order made by the Minister and published in the Gazette as comprised in the transfer pricing guidelines.'

The Gibraltar GAAR is triggered wherever a person enters into an 'arrangement' which is 'artificial or fictitious'. It operates by having the effect of reducing the amount of taxation payable. 'Arrangement' is defined in the ITA 2010 as an arrangement which enables any person to obtain a tax advantage, or such that the main benefit arising from the arrangement is a tax advantage and includes any scheme, transaction or series of transactions.[254] 'Artificial or fictitious', while not defined in the GAAR section, is defined in the general definitions section as meaning 'not real and not genuine, or not consistent with the international standards of the arm's length principle as defined by the OECD as part of its TP guidelines'.[255] Stemming from this section, the Income Tax Commissioner (the 'Commissioner') has the power to disregard the arrangement, or part of it, and reassess the correct amount of tax owed. Not only that, but as discussed earlier in the chapter, the Minister can then introduce legislation to strike down newly discovered loopholes.

Additionally, ITA 2010, ss 42 and 43 provides the taxpayer a level of certainty, by offering an advance clearance procedure (the notification regime briefly touched upon earlier in the chapter). This allows the taxpayer to have a proactive relationship with the Commissioner, and thus, as Gibraltar's then Chief Minister Sir Peter Caruana put it to Parliament in 2010, 'does not have to wait until he has done something to then find out whether he is going to be clobbered by the anti-avoidance provisions or not'.[256] Instead the Commissioner can assess the information and inform the taxpayer that the anti-avoidance provisions will be triggered against the particular arrangement reviewed, assuming that the taxpayer has been forthcoming and transparent with the information provided. Not only must the taxpayer be transparent in the submission of information, but the Commissioner and Income Tax Office — in accordance with the EU Code of Conduct Rules — must be transparent in making decisions publicly accessible for other taxpayers to benefit from similar factual matrices. As Caruana explained in the abovementioned speech before the Gibraltar Parliament , this 'cannot be private deal making between the taxing authority and the taxpayer... if the tax authority gives an advance ruling in favour of the taxpayer and the Commissioner believes that the ruling may have application to other tax payers, then he is obliged to publish the effect of that ruling, either in the form of guidance or in the form of a notice in the Gazette'.[257]

---

254 Income Tax Act 2010, ss 41(a) and 41(12)(a)

255 Income Tax Act 2010, s 74

256 Hansard 20th October 2010 page 38, para 1, Hansard 2010 (parliament.gi), accessed 5th July 2023

257 Ibid

Gibraltar GAAR: functionally weaker than other major GAARs?

The Commissioner must read and apply the Gibraltar GAAR alongside Article 9 of OECD's Model Tax Convention on Income and Capital[258] and all documents published by the OECD at any time before the implementation of the ITA 2010 as part of their Transfer Pricing guidelines[259]. In other words, the Commissioner and the Income Tax Office must have a deep understanding of the OECD's Model Tax Convention on Income and Capital and a deep understanding of the Transfer Pricing Guidelines. There is a risk therefore, that Gibraltar's GAAR which relies on a smaller tax administration,— like those of other small jurisdictions around the world — is bound to be functionally weaker than the GAARs of larger jurisdictions, such as the United Kingdom and Australia et al. This is the concern Waerzeggers raised when stating that 'the success of a GAAR in achieving its purpose will ultimately depend on (1) the legal design and drafting of the GAAR, and (2) the capacity of the tax authority to appropriately apply the GAAR in a measured, even handed and predictable way'.[260]

Following on from the administrative/resource challenges that the Commissioner may face, it can also be argued that the Gibraltar GAAR may be functionally weaker than other major GAARs due to its legislative construction. It is possible to argue that the Commissioner's powers under s 40(1) are negative in nature – in that the Commissioner's power is exercised by ignoring a transaction or step, not in making a positive action. For example, if a loan has no interest, the power under s 40(1) does not allow the Commissioner to introduce interest into the loan, rather simply to ignore the existence of the loan altogether.

However, such concerns can be refuted by the argument that, so long as the Commissioner and the Income Tax Office implement the rules in accordance with the TP guidelines and measurable OECD standards then the practical outcome should be satisfactory. Applied thus, the Gibraltar GAAR can be functionally as strong as the GAARs of other small jurisdictions worldwide.

---

258 Income Tax Act, s 40(b)

259 Income Tax Act, s 40(c)

260 Christophe Waerzeggers and Cory Hillier, 'Introducing a General Anti-Avoidance Rule (GAAR) [2016] 1(01) Tax Law IMF Technical Note 3

Gibraltar GAAR: needed by such a small jurisdiction?

The Gibraltar GAAR is necessary for such a small jurisdiction, as Caruana put it, 'to bring our tax system closer into the mainstream of conventional tax systems... and more acceptable to the international community, less of the sort required by more brass-plate tax-haven-type finance centre jurisdiction and more in keeping with the more mainstream onshore-type European financial services jurisdiction that Gibraltar has carefully tried to reposition itself towards in the last dozen years or so'.[261]

On a more general point, ensuring full compliance across the small jurisdiction of Gibraltar — and its limited resources — was enabled by the introduction of the Promoters' Notification Scheme under ITA 2010, s 41. This regime requires professional (coined 'promoters') to inform the Commissioner about 'arrangements' that have been put in place which 'enables... any person to obtain an advantage in relation to tax'.[262] The wording of promoter has been widely composed to catch any anyone designing, promoting, advising, recommending, or howsoever assisting the person implementing the arrangement'.[263] The arrangement has to be notified to the Commissioner within 30 days of the person with the reporting obligation making the proposal or becoming aware of it.[264] Legal professional privilege has been carved out.[265] As Caruana conveyed in his speech, 'this section [s 41] goes hand in hand with the ability to obtain advance rulings under section 42... in that it is just as much in the interests of a taxpayer to ensure that a scheme or arrangement is not going to be challenged on the basis of an advanced ruling, as it is in the interests of the Commissioner to be appraised of and close down aggressive schemes at the earliest opportunity.'[266]

261 Hansard 20th October 2010 page 27, para 1, Hansard 2010 (parliament.gi), accessed 5th July 2023

262 Income Tax Act 2010, Schedule 4, section 41(1)(a)(ii)

263 Income Tax Act 2010, Schedule 4, section 41(2)(a)(i)

264 Income Tax Act 2010, Schedule 4, section 41(3)

265 Income Tax Act 2010, Schedule 4, section 41(9)

266 Hansard Deb 2010 vol [add] page 40, para 1

The Gibraltar SAARs

As mentioned briefly earlier, the ITA 2010, s 40 not only provides a stronger intent and general regulation-making powers, but it also incorporates Schedule 4, which contains the Specific Anti-Avoidance Rules ('SAARs'), which we will now explore. Schedule 4 of the ITA starts by saying that 'in addition to the general provisions of s 40, the Commissioner may ascertain the taxation due from any person chargeable... in accordance with the provisions of this Schedule'.[267] The Gibraltar SAARs are an almost duplicate of the draft language produced by the OECD/G20. There has been very little deviation from them; however, it is useful to discuss and point out the Gibraltar-specific features where possible.

Thin Capitalisation

The first SAAR mentioned in the ITA 2010 in Schedule 4, Part 1 are the Thin Capitalisation rules ('Thin Cap'). The Thin Cap rules are triggered where, at any time in an accounting period, (a) the loan capital to equity ratio of a company (other than a credit institution or deposit taker regulated under the FSB) is greater than 5 to 1;[268] and (b) the company pays interest on a loan to a 'connected person' who/which is not a company and the loan is not considered to be at arm's length either of the rate of interest, or the terms and conditions of that loan.[269] For example, where a company has a loan capital of £1,500,000 on equity capital of £200,000, as this is greater than 5 to 1, the Thin Cap rules would be triggered under Sch 4, s 2.

A person is 'connected' with an 'individual' if that person is the individual's wife or husband, lives with him or her as if they were a wife or husband, or is a relative, or the wife or husband of a relative, of the individual, or of the individual's wife or husband.[270] A company is 'connected' to another company 'if the same person has control of both, or a person has control of one and persons connected

267 Income Tax Act 2010, Schedule 4, section 1

268 Income Tax Act 2010, Schedule 4, section 2(1)

269 Income Tax Act 2010, Schedule 4, section 2(1)(a)

270 Income Tax Act 2010, Schedule 4, section 9(2)

with him (as an individual or as a group)... have control of the other'.[271] 'Control' is roughly defined as being able to exercise or entitled to acquire, direct or indirect control over the company's affairs.[272] Caruana explains that the Thin Cap rules are the 'first in the context of a series of areas dealt with'.[273] The Gibraltar exception is that the Thin Cap rules are only applicable to loans made by 'non-companies'.[274]

Transactions with Connected Persons

The second SAAR mentioned in the ITA 2019 in Schedule 4, Part 2, s 4(1) are the rules on transactions with connected persons.

> 'Where a person carries on business with a connected person and it appears to the Commissioner that the course of business between those persons is so arranged, that the business done by the person chargeable to taxation in pursuance of his connection with the other person produces to the person either no profits, less than the ordinary profits, losses or increases the loss which might be expected to arise from that business, the person shall be assessable and chargeable to tax in respect of the profits which might be expected to arise from that business if it were transacted in accordance with the remainder of this Schedule'.[275]

The Commissioner will treat the interest in excess of what would have been paid to an arm's-length party as a non-deductible dividend.[276] Additionally, the law restricts deductibility of expenses paid to connected parties (as defined above).[277] Essentially, the aim of this part is to tackle what are termed 'transfer pricing abuses'. Caruana aptly explains this as 'the manipulation of profit by connected parties who are able to fix their pricing between each other or intervening parties, to

271 Income Tax Act 2010, Schedule 4, section 9(5)(a)(b) and 9(6)

272 Income Tax Act 2010, Schedule 4, section 10(1)

273 Hansard 20th October 2010 page 38 Hansard 2010 (parliament.gi)

274 Hansard 20th October 2010 page 38 Hansard 2010 (parliament.gi)

275 Income Tax Act 2010, Schedule 4, Part II, Section 4(1)

276 Income Tax Act 2010, Schedule 4, Part II, Section 4(2)

277 Income Tax Act 2010, Schedule 4, Part II, Section 4(3)

minimise their tax burden by leaving or dropping off the profits in the transaction in a lower tax jurisdiction.'[278] It is important to note that the TP rules incorporated in the ITA 2010 must be read and interpreted in a way which is compatible and consistent with the EU Code of Conduct and the OECD's Transfer Pricing Rules and continuing additional guidance. An example of the TP rules being triggered would be where, say, a subsidiary of XYZ Limited's parent borrows money at a significantly higher rate of interest than could have been obtained at arm's length by a non-connected lender, such as a recognisable bank. The execution of a comprehensive transfer pricing analysis is a complicated process, requiring an in-depth analysis of market conditions impacting that particular transaction (to give one example, the mere fact of a bank offering a lower interest rate need not automatically make that loan commercially more — or the most — viable for the company) all while analysing the OECD's TP rules and continuing guidance. There is a three-step exemption process available under the law, wherein it can be demonstrated that the avoidance of tax was either not the purpose or not the main purpose for which the transactions were effected.

Further confirmation of Gibraltar's long-standing commitment to tackling all forms of anti-avoidance can be found in the fact that the territory incorporated proto-Transfer Pricing ('TP') guidelines in the ITA 1952, s 49(2) verbatim from the Model Ordinance 1922, s 27(2), which provided:

> 'Where a non-resident person, not being a British subject, or a firm or company whose principal place of business is situated in His Majesty's Dominions or in territory under His Majesty's protection, or a branch thereof, carries on business with a resident person, and it appears to the Commissioner that owing to the close connection between the resident person and the non-resident person and to the substantial control exercised by the non-resident person over the resident person, the course of business between those persons can be so arranged and is so arranged, that the business done by the resident person in pursuance of his connection with the non-resident person produces to the resident person either no profits or less than the ordinary profits which might be expected to arise from that business, the non-resident person shall

278 Hansard 20th October 2010 page 39, para 1, Hansard 2010 (parliament.gi), accessed 5th July 2023

be assessable and chargeable to tax in the name of the resident person as if the resident person were an agent of the non-resident person.'

It can be argued that this is a primitive version of modern-day TP guidelines, aiming to tackle non-arm-length transactions between connected parties, and further highlighting Gibraltar's firm and deep-footed stance of tackling and producing legislation to tackle avoidance.

Transfer of Assets Abroad

The third SAAR mentioned in the ITA 2010 Part 4 of Schedule 4 deals with the transfer of assets abroad. This section tackles the transfer of assets abroad where the income derived from them subsequently falls outside the remit of the existing legislation. Caruana in his speech explained that s 12 introduces the protection of 'imposing taxation on income arising to a foreign entity which results from a transfer of assets abroad by an ordinarily resident taxpayer and which is or would be available to the ordinarily resident taxpayer.'[279] Furthermore, this part 'also applies to capital sums arising from the transfer which can be matched with income which arises before or after to the foreign entity.'[280] The income would be taxable if that income would have been taxed in Gibraltar, had it originally stemmed from Gibraltar. The transfer of assets abroad regime will not be triggered, if it can be shown that avoiding tax liability was not the purpose, or the main purpose for which the transfers were effected.[281]

he TOAA regime is something of an oddity in Gibraltar, as it is most likely that assets will flow into the jurisdictions rather than out. Arguably, while tax rates remain low – something which will likely be the case in the short-medium term –this will not be the most deployed SAAR. That said, we can see some indication of how it may work practically, due to the appeal decision in the well-known case of *HMRC v Fisher*[282]. In this case, the Court of Appeal held that the

279 Hansard 20th October 2010 page 39, para 2, Hansard 2010 (parliament.gi), accessed 5th July 2023 and Income Tax Act 2010, Schedule 4, Part 4, Section 12(1)

280 Ibid

281 Income Tax Act 2010, Schedule 4, Part 4, Section 12(2)(b)

282 *HMRC v Fisher and others* [2021] EWCA Civ 1438

UK's TOAA regime applied to assets transferred to Gibraltar in regard to two of the three shareholders, and that profits were subject to income tax in the UK. Specifically, the Court of Appeal held that the regime could be triggered where the transfer is actioned by a minority shareholder voting in favour of a particular matter. Additionally, where any commercial reasoning is 'too' closely linked to the tax minimisation strategy, then the motive defence can be disregarded. The Fishers appealed this decision to the UK Supreme Court and in November 2023, the Supreme Court held in the taxpayers' favour, and unanimously decided that the individual who is liable to the primary charge is the one who makes the transfer of assets abroad. Furthermore, the Supreme Court held that the transfer of assets by a company is not to be treated as a transfer by the shareholders or directors.

Corporate Interest Limitation Rule

The fourth SAAR is the Corporate Interest Limitation Rule found in Part 5 of Schedule 4, which aims to limit the amount of borrowing costs which can be deducted during the tax period in which they can be incurred.[283] 'Exceeding borrowing costs incurred by a taxpayer shall be deductible in the tax period in which they are incurred only up to the greater of the following two amounts: (a) 30% of the taxpayer's EBITDA; or (b) €3,000,000'[284] (considered for the entire group). [285]The law has carved out an exemption for 'loans used to finance a long-term public infrastructure project, where the project operator, borrowing costs, assets and revenues are all within the EU'.[286] This SAAR is almost identical to the ATAD wording and as such it does not count as legislation unique to Gibraltar.

Exit Taxation

The fifth SAAR is the Exit Taxation regime and is covered in Part 6 of Schedule 4. Its purpose being to impose a tax on unrealised capital gains when companies

283 Income Tax Act 2010, Schedule 4, Part 5, Section 18(3)

284 Income Tax Act 2010, Schedule 4, Part 5, Section 18(3)(a)(b)

285 Income Tax Act 2010, Schedule 4, Part 5, Section 18(4)

286 Income Tax Act 2010, Schedule 4, Part 5, Section 18(6)(b)

migrate their tax residency or transfer assets offshore. If that is the case, then the taxpayer will be charged to tax on the amount equal to the market value of the transferred assets which would otherwise have produced assessable income at the time of the assets' migration.[287] Market value is defined as 'the amount for which an asset can be exchanged or mutual obligations can be settled between willing unrelated buyers and sellers in a direct transaction'.[288] The law provides a carve-out whereby 'asset transfers related to the financing of securities, assets posted as collateral or where the asset transfer takes place in order to meet prudential capital requirements or for the purpose of liquidity management'.[289] This SAAR is almost identical to the ATAD wording and nothing of further significance can be said about it from a uniquely Gibraltar perspective, other than that it applies only to Gibraltar-assessable income.

Controlled Foreign Company Rules

The sixth SAAR is Controlled Foreign Company Rules ('CFC') and these are covered in Part 7 of Schedule 4 with the purpose of minimising the incentive to move profit from its home jurisdiction into a low-tax, foreign jurisdiction. A CFC means an 'entity or a permanent establishment' not resident in Gibraltar which is held by a Gibraltar ordinarily resident taxpayer:[290] (i) with 50% of voting rights; or (ii) owns 50% of capital; or (iii) has a right to receive 50% of profits;[291] AND the entity or permanent establishment pays less than 50% of the tax which would have been paid had the taxable event occurred in Gibraltar.[292] If this test is satisfied, then 'the non-distributed income of the company or permanent establishment arising from non-genuine arrangements which have been put in place for the essential purpose of obtaining a tax advantage shall be included as income of the taxpayer for that tax period'.[293]

287 Income Tax Act 2010, Schedule 4, Part 5, Section 18A(2)

288 Income Tax Act 2010, Schedule 4, Part 5, Section 18A(9)

289 Income Tax Act 2010, Schedule 4, Part 5, Section 18A(10)

290 Income Tax Act 2010, Schedule 4, Part 5, Section 19(1)(a)

291 Income Tax Act 2010, Schedule 4, Part 5, Section 19(1)(a)(i)(ii)(iii)

292 Income Tax Act 2010, Schedule 4, Part 5, Section 19(1)(b)

293 Income Tax Act 2010, Schedule 4, Part 5, Section 19(2)

Hybrid Mismatch

The Hybrid Mismatch rules is the final SAAR, covered in Part 8 of Schedule 4.[294] The rules aim to prevent the exploitation of differences between tax systems to obtain double non-taxation/deductions/deductions without inclusions and non-taxation without inclusion. The rules were incorporated into the ITA 2010 as part of the OECD's BEPS Project. Differences in how jurisdictions characterise taxable events can enable taxpayers to take advantage of the anomalies. For example, one jurisdiction might characterise the payment from one to another as a dividend under the category of non-taxable events, while another jurisdiction might define that as interest and therefore enable deductions against it. This SAAR is almost identical to the ATAD wording and as such it does not count as legislation unique to Gibraltar.

Taxation Agreement between Spain and the UK regarding Gibraltar

While not a GAAR or a SAAR, at the heart of the new International Agreement on Taxation between Spain and the United Kingdom regarding Gibraltar ("Gib-Spain Agreement") is the drive to tackle tax avoidance. Not only that, its divergence from an off-the-shelf OECD double taxation treaty makes it unique to analyse. While it is outside the remit of this chapter, it has been evaluated elsewhere in this book.

Conclusion

This chapter has demonstrated that Gibraltar's 'culture of compliance' did not just come about with the introduction of the ITA 2010 and the EU-wide compliance push; instead, Gibraltar has had a tax system with anti-avoidance at its core for well over a hundred years. A tax system designed to prevent against its abuse right from the beginning with the proto-GAAR and proto–TP Rules. A rich and deep history of embracing unequivocal anti-avoidance legislative frameworks. A rigorous system to ensure that the majority of taxpayers do not bear the burden

294 Income Tax Act 2010, Schedule 4, Part 5, Sections 21-28

of avoidance created by the minority who do not pay. This chapter has explored the broader developments of the GAAR before analysing the Gibraltar GAAR in detail, and subsequently analysing the Gibraltar SAARs, from, where possible, a uniquely Gibraltar perspective. As long as the GAAR and SAARs are executed by the Income Tax Office and its Commissioner of Income Tax in accordance with the standard guidelines, then Gibraltar shall remain firmly in the mainstream of conventional tax systems in its approach to tackling avoidance.

Editor's Note as to Pillar 2 Implementation

On 11 July 2023 the Chief Minister, Fabian Picardo, announced Gibraltar would implement the Pillar 2 section of the GloBE Tax Challenges Arising from the Digitalisation of the Economy Rules, which were published by the OECD following the 8 October 2021 Statement on a Two-Pillar Solution to Address the Tax Challenges Arising from the Digitalisation of the Economy[295], for accounting periods beginning no earlier than 1 January 2025.

However, on 19 December 2023[296] the Gibraltar Government announced a two-stage approach to implementation which would begin on 1 January 2024 with what is described as 'Minimum Top-Up Tax on Gibraltar Resident Subsidiaries'(MTTGS) which when implemented will have the effect of levying a Qualified Domestic Minimum Top-Up Tax only on those subsidiaries of foreign headquartered MNE groups with a qualifying income of €750m or more.

At the time of writing, there is little detail, other than that the MTTGS will meet the relevant tests to be a QDMTT where applicable, and that it will be subject to a revision or repeal once a wider implementation of Pillar 2 is introduced in twelve months, according to the original timetable given by the Chief Minister in his Budget Address.

Implementation of Pillar 2 is entirely consistent with the argument presented in this chapter that Gibraltar has been and remains an early adopter, where

295 See Statement on a Two-Pillar Solution to Address the Tax Challenges Arising from the Digitalisation of the Economy – 8 October 2021 - OECD

296 Pillar Two Qualified Domestic Minimum Top-Up Tax OECD/G20 Base Erosion and Profit Shifting Project - 878/2023 (gibraltar.gov.gi)

possible, of anti-avoidance provisions, and that by doing so, it cements its position as a highly compliant participant in the current round of international tax reform.

Chapter 7

SPAIN IS REAL AND CANNOT BE IGNORED

Grahame Jackson and Isaac Levy

Introduction

It can be assumed that nearly all readers of this work are aware of the territorial dispute surrounding the existence of Gibraltar, and the fact that it is inextricably linked to its near neighbour, Spain. Nearly all readers will also acknowledge that much has been written about the rights and wrongs of this dispute and that a book on the principles of taxation is not the place to elaborate on the geo-political position of Gibraltar. However, since this position can and does have bearing on matters of tax law, and should you require further detail, we refer you to the other parts of this book wherein the historic position of Gibraltar is discussed, and we ask you to bear the dispute in mind when reading this chapter.

Regardless of those differing perspectives, Gibraltar is not an island: it sits within its geographic context, the relationship with Spain and the Spanish hinterland is vital to Gibraltar, with much of the latter's workforce commuting into the territory on a daily basis,[297] and the territory's proximity to Spain informs much of the policy agenda, simply due to its physical presence. A fitting example can be found within the area of tax policy: 1952 saw the introduction of income tax in Gibraltar, in an Act drafted specifically to take into account Gibraltar's distinct geographic identity as a peninsula. In the early to mid-twentieth century the United Kingdom was still considered a world power, with overseas territories from Gibraltar to Hong Kong, and demonstrably stronger than Spain, which was recovering from a bloody civil war and the final death throes of its own, once-global empire. That was the context into which the Income Tax Act 1952 was introduced, but in the intervening years, the balance between the two nations has

---

297 HM Gibraltar Govt statistics state that in December 2022 there were 15,106 'frontier workers'; that is, those listed as being resident in Spain, but working in Gibraltar

become much more level. As Britain's 'colonies' became 'dependencies' (in 1982) and then 'overseas territories' (in 2002), there has been a concomitant devolution of responsibility towards locally elected governments,[298] and the Empire has been reduced to a mere 14 territories with a population of 272,000.[299] Over the same period, specifically in Gibraltar the character of the jurisdiction has changed greatly with the shift away from Ministry of Defence spending as the majority of the economy.[300] Freed of the need to service the garrison, Gibraltar has developed an economy which faces the hinterland, drawing not only labour but also expertise from its surroundings. These changes may modify the concerns of those writing tax law, but there is one constant underlying problem, that of international mobility and the interaction of the tax laws of Spain and Gibraltar. If Gibraltar gives no heed to the proximity of Spain and the ease of travel to and from it, then it will either damage its own tax base (if it is concerned with leakage in the direction of Spain) or affects the tax base of Spain (if leakage is in the opposite direction). Neither of these two outcomes is sustainable in the current era.

The two solutions offered by the current provisions and the 1952 Act betray the difference in concern between the two eras: in 1952 the concern seems to have been for a loss of tax base in the direction of Spain, while the current provisions deal with matters in the opposite direction. However, both are driven by the necessity of accepting Spain's existence, accepting Spain's proximity, and accepting that movement across the border is easier than some tax officials might wish it to be. In this chapter, we will explore the two methods used to deal with that problem, firstly by discussing the provision in the 1952 Act, and latterly by the 2019 Agreement, more commonly known as the 'Tax Treaty'.[301]

---

298 For example, Gibraltar has had four constitutions since 1950 (1950, 1964, 1969 and 2006) each more devolved than the last.

299 'Global Britain and the British Overseas Territories: Resetting the Relationship', Fifteenth Report of the Session 2017 – 19, House of Commons 2019

300 Whilst statistics prior to 1987 are not easy to source, a strong indication of the effect of the removal of UK defence spending is that HM Dockyard accounted for 2,532 workers from a work force of 12,507 across Gibraltar in 1987, compared to 295 in the year 2000 (see p34 Abstract of Statistics 1987 compared to p28 Abstract of Statistics 2001, both Government of Gibraltar)

301 Otherwise known as the International Agreement on Taxation and the Protection of

The 1952 Act – Residence as anti-avoidance

The 1952 Act, as has been repeatedly referenced throughout this work, is a descendant of the Model Income Tax Ordinance published as an annex to the report of the Interdepartmental Committee on Income Tax in the Colonies Not Possessing Responsible Government.[302] That model takes an essentially territorial approach to taxation and in regard to individuals, it does not contain a definition of residence which would be recognisable to those who work in today's taxation environment. In regard to a company, the Act does go some way towards an effective definition of residence:

> ' "Company" means any company incorporated or registered under any law in force in the Colony, and any company which though incorporated or registered outside the Colony, carries on business or has an office or place of business therein.'[303]

In other words, a company is not within the definition of 'company' unless it is either registered in the relevant colony or trades there. By the time of the repeal of the 1952 Act, this definition had been split into two: firstly the definition of company itself had been widened to include any company incorporated or registered anywhere in the world, and secondly a discrete definition of 'ordinarily resident' had been inserted and widened to include:

> '"ordinarily resident" when applied to a company -
> a. a company, the management and control of whose business is exercised in Gibraltar; or
> b. a company which carries on business in Gibraltar and the management and control of which is exercised outside Gibraltar by persons ordinarily

---

Financial Interests between the Kingdom of Spain and the United Kingdom of Great Britain and Northern Ireland regarding Gibraltar entered into on 4th March 2019

302 Report of the Interdepartmental Committee on Income Tax in the Colonies not possessing responsible government, HM Stationery Office 1922

303 ibid Appendix I - s2 Model Income Tax Ordinance

resident within the meaning of this Act...'[304]

The need for some sort of formally articulated test for tax residence in regard to a company and an individual arises partly as a result of the introduction of the first League of Nations Model Treaty for the Elimination of Double Taxation, which arose from the recommendations of the Committee of Experts on Double Taxation and Tax Evasion and was published in 1928.[305] This model treaty is the ancestor of all other model treaties which have followed, and it establishes the modern international taxation system. It functions by establishing the country of residence of a person as the default place of taxation on a worldwide basis, with taxing rights to income of different types allocated between the jurisdiction of source and the jurisdiction of residence, with a system of double taxation relief between the two.[306] However, one can identify the concerns of a jurisdiction whose highly mobile population can easily leave and return.

The s2 1952 Act definition of tax residence follows the traditional common law test of tax residence as articulated in *De Beers Consolidated Mines Ltd v Howe* [1906] AC 455, which was developed from the work of German jurist Friedrich Carl von Savigny.[307] However, it adds an element which is absent from the De Beers definition, in that it makes provision for a company to be resident in Gibraltar by virtue of its management and control being exercised outside Gibraltar by persons who are themselves ordinarily resident in Gibraltar. This is a clear recognition of the ease with which a group of directors could pass across the

304 s2 Income Tax Act 1952

305 League of Nations Double Taxation and Tax Evasion Report Presented by the General Meeting of the Government Experts on Double Taxation and Tax Evasion – League of Nations Draft Model treaty (1928)

306 For a discussion of the wider need for a test of tax residence in the modern era see Jackson, G. 'The Utility of Tax Residence Tests beyond Taxing Rights and the Concept of "Tests of Belonging" Given the Growing Number of Multilateral Provisions in the Context of Territorial Tax Regimes' Bulletin for International Taxation 2022 (Volume 76) No 6

307 J. F. Avery Jones & J. Hattingh *De Beers Consolidated Mines Ltd v Howe* (1906) Corporate Residence: An Early Attempt at European Harmonisation (2020)

border to La Linea or similar places within easy reach in the Campo de Gibraltar, thereby avoiding tax residence under the 1952 Act and the charge contained in s6(3) of the 1952 Act which was applicable to companies on a global basis. As Gibraltar continues to have a management-only test for corporate residence in the 2010 Act, this anti-avoidance provision finds a mirror in s74 of the 2010 Act which uses identical language.

The 1952 Act also includes a 'bespoke' definition of the term 'ordinarily resident', which seems motivated by a similar urge to tax those who flow easily across the border between Spain and Gibraltar. In order to set this in context, one must understand that the 1922 Model Ordinance was concerned primarily with the inter-relations of British territories and Empire subjects. For example, at s46 of the 1922 Model Ordinance, one finds a section devoted to the relief of double taxation. This section applies only to relief of tax paid to either the United Kingdom or other parts of the Empire. The interaction of what could be called 'British' or 'Empire taxation' and the taxation of third countries is not properly dealt with. An echo of this can be seen in the definition of 'ordinarily resident' as applicable to an individual, contained at s2 of the 1952 Act;

> '"ordinarily resident", when applied to an individual, means an individual who, irrespective of whether such individual is domiciled in Gibraltar or otherwise, resides in Gibraltar except for such temporary absences as to the Commissioner may seem reasonable and not inconsistent with the claim of such person to be ordinarily resident, and includes an individual who is a British subject or a citizen of the Republic of Ireland who is employed or self-employed in Gibraltar and who resides wholly within the Campo district or partly within Gibraltar and partly within that district, except for such temporary absences as aforesaid (the Campo district for this purpose being the areas comprised within the former Consular Districts of Her Majesty's Vice-Consulates at La Linea and Algeciras as they existed immediately prior to the abolition of those Vice-Consulates).

It is firstly interesting to note that this definition makes no reference to a day count. It establishes a two-tier residence test:

i. 'For all nationalities one must reside in Gibraltar (with no definition of "resides" in the statute); and

ii. For British or Republic of Ireland persons then if you have employment or self-employment in Gibraltar and reside within a reasonable distance of Gibraltar.'

Under the 1952 Act a Spaniard living in La Linea is not 'ordinarily resident' in Gibraltar, but a person from Dublin or Liverpool is. In other words, those who are connected by passport[308] to the territory are subject to ordinary residence, even if they would not otherwise be, if they are geographically proximate to it. As with limb (b) of the ordinary residence test for companies in the 1952 Act, this would seem to be a provision which could loosely be seen as part of the 1952 Act's anti-avoidance measures. A British subject should not be permitted to escape British Gibraltarian tax simply by living in Spain, just as a company subject to Gibraltar law in its incorporation (being thus, in effect, a British subject) should not be able to escape tax residence simply by virtue of holding its meetings across the border in La Linea.

The 2010 Act – a moderated bespoke provision

The 2010 Act discarded the unique and bespoke residence definition contained in s2 of the 1952 Act. Instead, it chose to take a more standard approach to the definition of personal ordinary residence whilst essentially retaining the corporate residence test. Now located in s74, the definition of personal ordinary residence was recast to state:

'"ordinarily resident" when applied to an individual means an individual who irrespective of whether such individual is domiciled in Gibraltar or otherwise who in any year of assessment–

a. is present in Gibraltar for a period of, or periods together amounting to, at least 183 days; or

308 It is important to remember that until 1949 the Republic of Ireland had an ambiguous status and that citizens of the Republic of Ireland were not regarded as 'aliens' under British nationality. This hybrid status continues today and would explain the inclusion of Republic of Ireland citizens in s2 of the 1952 Act.

b. is present in Gibraltar in any year of assessment which is one of three consecutive years in which the total of the days on which the individual is present in Gibraltar exceeds 300, and for the purposes of this definition presence in Gibraltar for any part of a 24-hour period commencing at midnight shall be counted as a day of presence whether or not any accommodation is used in Gibraltar;'

Limb (a) of the personal test mirrors the test common to many European jurisdictions. Limb (b) is a less usual affair and whilst one cannot be certain, it would seem to be a response to the back-and-forth movements of those across the border with continuing connection to Gibraltar. One feature of note in limb (b) is that it merely applies to three 'consecutive years' and not to three consecutive years retrospectively. Therefore, in the situation that a person has 199 days in Year 1 and 100 days in Year 2, they cannot know their residence status in Year 2 until the completion of Year 3, in a sense they become Schrödinger's Tax Resident, whose status is variable depending on when they ask the question.

Finally, for the purposes of the day count for personal residence, the classification of 'any presence' as a whole day indicates strongly the authorities' awareness that large proportions of the workforce reside in Spain and travel into Gibraltar. In effect it ensures, for the purposes of the 2010 Act, that those who reside in Spain but work in Gibraltar become tax resident in Gibraltar. In the same fashion, the geographic element of the 1952 Act applies such residence to British nationals in the Campo. In the 2010 Act, all nationals who work in Gibraltar for a number of days above 183 (which will functionally mean those who reside in the Campo) are subject to Gibraltar tax residence. It has the same effect, but on all nationalities.

The 2010 Act coincided with a general drop in the rates of tax applicable to individuals. In 2003 the rate of tax for those with more than £15000 in taxable income was 45%,[309] falling to 40% over £16000 in 2008,[310] and in 2010 the Gross Income Based system was introduced as an alternative tax model with a lower burden for those without numerous allowances. The overall effect was to increase the disparity between personal tax in Gibraltar and that in Spain (with Gibraltar charging less).

309 Rates of Tax (Amendment) Rules 2003 Rule 2(2)

310 Rates of Tax Rules (Amendment) Rules 2008 Rule 2(2)

The Tax Treaty – a responsible neighbour

In the world of 1952 and in fact in the world of 2000 there was no international framework which was available to jurisdictions such as Gibraltar to actively take a role in seeking to eliminate tax avoidance across borders. Conceptually jurisdictions as small as Gibraltar were not operating within a community of jurisdictions, but instead utilising their tax sovereignty in isolation of other jurisdictions. Just as the framers of the 1922 Model Ordinance had not sought to eliminate double taxation outside the British Empire, the legislators of the mid- to late-20th century understood taxation systems as discrete; given which, in the 1969 Constitution, responsibility for taxation measures rested with the devolved Government of Gibraltar, while the collection of taxes and enforcement remained the remit of the Financial and Development Secretary[311]. The exercise of tax sovereignty, therefore, came relatively late to the devolved Government of Gibraltar. As the territory has grown and developed as an international jurisdiction, its approach has been modified to play a part in the international community of nations, and to present itself, not as a territory devoid of relations to others and exercising the powers devolved to it in isolation, but as a good and responsible neighbour. This mirrors a wider, global change in approach to tax cooperation and neighbourliness, which some have characterised as a change in the very nature of sovereignty: away from the traditional Westphalian model towards an understanding of Sovereignty as Responsibility.[312] Debate persists as to whether this amounts to a change in sovereignty itself or merely a change in the use of the sovereign power, but it is beyond doubt that the approach of governments and jurisdictions has changed across the globe. It is furthermore true that the devolved governments of overseas territories such as Gibraltar understand the ways in which their actions in the tax arena have consequences, for which they are responsible not only to their sovereign 'mother country' but also to the wider international community.[313]

---

311 Despatch of 23rd May 1969, Governor Admiral of the Fleet Sir Varyl Begg to the Foreign and Commonwealth Office on the entry into force of the Gibraltar Constitution Order 1969.

312 See Chapter 4, Dietsch 2015

313 For a wider discussion of Gibraltar's compliance with international obligations see Chapter 5.

Originally this move away from tax sovereignty exercised in isolation came as a consequence of Gibraltar being an EU territory between 1971 and 2020. Gibraltar implemented the gamut of EU Directives in the tax field and was also subject to a number of European Court of Justice cases around its tax legislation. As a consequence of this, by 2020 Gibraltar had a taxation system which had retained the principles of the 1922 Model Ordinance, but which had also been subject to the scrutiny of the EU Commission, of the Court of Justice of the European Union and of the EU Code of Conduct in Business Taxation Group. For example, as a result of EU scrutiny around State Aid and the Code of Conduct in Business Taxation in 2013, Gibraltar introduced the Class 1 A charge on inter-company interest. Despite this the Spanish authorities had maintained Gibraltar on their domestic list of non-cooperative jurisdictions for tax purposes, imposing a withholding tax on all payments to Gibraltar of 35%. It is not for this article to discuss the mismatch between the EU's approach and that of the Spanish authorities. However, it was apparent that the UK's withdrawal from the European Union would place Gibraltar and its economy on a worse footing: lacking the status as an EU territory, and subject to a territorial claim from Spain. A form of cooperation is envisaged by Article 3(1) of the Protocol on Gibraltar to the UK's Withdrawal Agreement and the Memoranda of Understanding that cover various other areas are also envisaged by similar articles to the Protocol. It was this vision of cross border relations that led in 2019 to the UK — with Gibraltar's participation — negotiating what became known as the Tax Treaty. In his note on the Parliamentary Resolution for the Introduction of Gazette Notice to Implement Tax Treaty with Spain 165/2021, Chief Minister Fabian Picardo explained the needs for the treaty, and it is worth quoting a large section to articulate the thoughts of the government at the time:

> 'Our departure from the EU prompted a change in Spain's historic and relentless approach towards Gibraltar. Despite having maintained this approach for the better part of 30 years, Spain demonstrated a willingness to engage constructively in addressing cross-border tax issues.
>
> The conclusion of the Treaty marks an important and positive move towards establishing these closer relations and is an inevitable and welcome first step. It is commonplace between neighbouring states with a high volume of cross-border traffic, flows and common interests.
>
> The Treaty enables both sides to cooperate with each other similarly to the

way each does with their other treaty partners around the world. This spirit of co-operation and understanding is necessary given the close economic and social ties between Gibraltar and Spain.

It is nevertheless important to understand the outcome in the context of the journey made. Spain had serious misconceptions about both Gibraltar's tax system and its commitment to tax transparency. In addition, it was necessary to unravel many years of prejudice driven primarily by the continuous propagation of myths regarding a lack of adequate standards in relation to international tax compliance and good governance, not to mention the classification of Gibraltar as a tax haven by Spain.

Spain considers the Gibraltar tax act to be one that facilitates the evasion of taxes in Spain. This is the reason Spain has not only blacklisted Gibraltar, but also embarked on an aggressive policy of seeking to get other countries and international organisations to similarly blacklist or sanction Gibraltar. Whilst this policy has only had limited impact, it has nonetheless created a degree of uncertainty internationally regarding the tax system in Gibraltar and blocked Gibraltar's progress. The intensity and extent of this uncertainty has "ebbed and flowed" with the level of scrutiny and review that the tax act in Gibraltar has, over many years, been subjected to in the form of a European Union State Aid investigation, comprising numerous court cases and high-level technical reviews.

In negotiating this Treaty, Gibraltar has sought to carefully navigate and manage these expectations providing an opportunity to understand Spain's concerns and the misconceptions they had about the tax system in Gibraltar. It has allowed these issues to be addressed in the most effective manner possible without eroding its taxing rights.'[314]

So, Gibraltar's aim in negotiating the Tax Treaty was to protect the position it had acquired as an EU territory from erosion by an aggressive Spain. In a post-Brexit arena, a Spain pulling at the levers of power in the various international organisations, motivated by an urge to advance its territorial claims was Gibraltar's worst-case scenario, and this necessitated a tax treaty as part of wider negotiations

314 Paras 22 – 27 Chief Minister's note on Parliamentary Resolution for the Introduction of Gazette Notice to Implement Tax Treaty with Spain - 165/2021 (gibraltar.gov.gi)

for the future relationship with the EU. Ultimately, this gave rise to the Tax Treaty, entered into on the 4th March 2019.

The Provisions of the Tax Treaty

When understanding the Tax Treaty, one must first acknowledge that it is an entirely unique document. It follows no model form, and though it does mirror some language of international treaties and the OECD Model Convention on Income and on Capital, it should be understood as a creature unto itself. It does not deal with the normal matters of double taxation and cannot truly be called a 'Double Taxation Treaty', instead one could possibly better characterise it as an Anti-Avoidance Treaty, in that it seems designed to eliminate opportunities for avoidance by Spanish nationals and residents using Gibraltar entities or the tax jurisdiction of Gibraltar. Its aim is to do the opposite of the provisions regarding residence in the 1952 Act, ensuring that Spain can still tax those Spanish nationals utilising Gibraltar as a jurisdiction, whether for residence or for the organisation of enterprises. Whilst it is lengthier and more comprehensive, it is identifiably the converse of the s2 definitions of 'ordinarily resident' in the 1952 Act.

Spain's aim is well summed up on the Chief Minister's Note of 26th February 2021;

> 'Spain's paramount concern was the perceived loss of tax revenue from Spain to Gibraltar. Gibraltar is the lower tax jurisdiction. It has tax rates that are substantially lower than those in Spain and does not impose taxes on capital, wealth or savings income. Complex cross-border structures can therefore be used to exploit advantages and opportunities of double non-taxation. This is compounded further given the relative ease in moving from one jurisdiction to the other.
>
> This is the mischief that Spain aims to prevent in the Treaty. Spain no longer pursues any wider agenda regarding Gibraltar's taxation system. It focuses on their immediate and close concerns and the best way in which to address them.'[315]

315 *Ibid* para 30-31

Just as with the definitions of 'ordinarily resident', the ease of cross border movement is a factor missing in ordinary treaties regarding taxation.

When understanding the provisions of the Tax Treaty, one should perhaps deal with the articles in the order they are presented. Little academic work has been carried out on the Tax Treaty, though a large amount of commercial commentary has been produced (some by the authors). We will proceed by highlighting those articles which we believe are of importance: each article will be discussed in turn, quoting those parts of the Article which we believe require highlighting and then an overall comment will be made after such discussion. We will not be attempting a line-by-line analysis of the Tax Treaty, to do so would require a detailed work in itself and we encourage our fellow tax professionals to undertake such an analysis. In our commentary, we have quoted the documentation issued by the Gibraltar Government and the Income Tax Office. We would caution against over-reliance on these documents, no guidance has been issued by the Spanish authorities, and we are conscious of the legal status of guidance. Guidance is not law and though it may be issued by an authority cannot be read as such. It is exactly what it says it is, guidance. Given the unique nature of much of the language in the Tax Treaty, litigation on both sides of the border may be required if we are to be given truly definitive interpretations. We have therefore, treated such documents as important, but not definitive.

Article 1 – Protection of financial interests and tax good governance

> '(1) All the legislation and standards of the European Union as regards transparency, administrative cooperation, harmful tax practices and antimony laundering shall continue to be applied in Gibraltar until the date on which EU law ceases to apply in Gibraltar.
>
> (2) From the date on which EU law ceases to apply in Gibraltar, legislation equivalent to EU legislation which exists on that date shall be maintained in Gibraltar.'

Commentary

This article provides guarantees as to the continued application of EU law during the continuation of Gibraltar's status as an EU territory (1(1)). With regard to Article 1(2) it must be read in its context and that is that the Tax Treaty deals with matters tax related. Therefore, it commits Gibraltar to maintain legislation equivalent to that which is in force on the date of exit from the EU in regard to tax matters There must be no back sliding of standards. It does not commit Gibraltar to any new legislation.

Article 2 – Tax Residency

Article 2 (1) – Natural Persons

Natural persons

'(1) For the purposes of this Agreement, the Parties agree that:

(a) Natural persons shall be tax resident in Spain or in Gibraltar in accordance with their domestic law, including rules regarding the issuance of tax certificates confirming residency and subject to the following rules only in cases of tax residency conflicts;

(b) Where, by reason of the provisions in paragraph (1)(a) natural persons are resident of both Parties then their status shall be determined as follows:

i. Natural persons shall be tax resident only in Spain when any of the following circumstances exist:

   A. They spend over 183 overnight stays of the calendar year in Spain. In determining the count of overnight stays, sporadic absences in neither Spain nor Gibraltar shall be added to the time where these individuals spend the majority of their overnight stays;
   B. In the event that, pursuant to the Spanish tax legislation, their spouse (from whom they are not legally separated) or the natural person with whom a similar relationship has been established, and/or any dependent ascendants or descendants, resides or reside habitually in Spain;
   C. The only permanent home at their disposal is in Spain; or
   D. Two thirds of their net assets, determined pursuant to Spanish Tax legislation, whether held directly or indirectly, are located in Spain;

ii. When the provisions of paragraph (1)(b)(i) are not conclusive, natural persons shall be considered tax residents only in Spain, unless they are able to provide reliable evidence that they have a permanent home for their exclusive use in Gibraltar and remain in Gibraltar over 183 days;'

Commentary

At first glance, this article 2(1) appears to be a simple tie-breaker in the manner of Article 4 of the OECD Model Convention on Income and on Capital (2017). However, there are certain key differences which themselves illustrate the varying concerns of the creators of the Model Convention and Article 2(1).

Firstly, it is worthy of note that, as with Article 2(1), Article 4 is applicable only where a person is tax resident in both jurisdictions. This is possible because, when calculating days present for the purposes of their domestic tax residence test, both jurisdictions count any presence as a day. In other words, a person who travels regularly between Gibraltar and Spain will have a scenario where they will double count days (that is one day in Gibraltar and one day in Spain in a single calendar day) when they are partly in both jurisdictions. Article 2(1)(a) protects the domestic legislation of both parties as the starting point, as does Article 4. However, unlike Article 4, Article 2(1)(b)(i) is framed to apply the tiebreaker tests in the favour of Spanish residence in all cases. Article 2(1) does not lay out a test whereby a person is treated solely as Gibraltar tax resident. However, despite the impression this may give, there is a 'Gibraltar' possible result, Article 2(1)(b)(ii) states that:

> (ii) When the provisions of paragraph (1)(b)(i) are not conclusive, natural persons shall be considered tax residents only in Spain, unless they are able to provide reliable evidence that they have a permanent home for their exclusive use in Gibraltar and remain in Gibraltar over 183 days;

Therefore, if all of the tiebreakers are exhausted and the individual can prove reliably that they are present in Gibraltar for 183 days in a given year and they have a permanent home for their exclusive use, then they will be treated as Gibraltar resident.

Article 4 of the Model Convention on Income and Capital lays out a test for identifying which of the two parties to the Model Convention has the better claim to tax residence. In contrast Article 2(1) applies a series of tests which are designed to determine if a person is resident solely in Spain, with a Gibraltar-relevant test only being applicable as a back-stop. This approach underpins our conclusion that the Tax Treaty is in its characteristics an anti-avoidance treaty, rather than a double taxation treaty. As the Chief Minister said;

> 'Gibraltar is the lower tax jurisdiction. It has tax rates that are substantially lower than those in Spain and does not impose taxes on capital, wealth or savings income.'[316]

Given the lower rates of tax in Gibraltar and the more limited tax base, then if one were seeking to avoid tax, it would make no sense to become tax resident in Spain. There is no need for a tie-breaker to work in Gibraltar's favour. In other words, the mischief which was such an issue in the 1952 Act (of British nationals 'hiding' from tax in Spain) is now no longer the issue; instead the issue as highlighted by the Chief Minister is tax avoidance and/or evasion in the opposite direction. This is somewhat supported by the contents of the Frequently Asked Question (FAQs) International Tax Agreement: Gibraltar – Spain issued by HM Government of Gibraltar Income Tax Office in November 2021 (the FAQs) which states;

> 'The Treaty does not favour or give an advantage to Spain. It allocates taxing rights to the contracting state with the emphasis on residency-based taxation and therefore the greater need to determine residency. This presumption clearly demonstrates the difference in the tax basis between Gibraltar and Spain. Spain needs to establish tax residency in order to tax an individual, whilst Gibraltar does not require tax residency to tax an individual's income. This is the reason why there is less focus on proving residency in Gibraltar and a greater focus and emphasis the other way around.
>
> It is the rebuttal of this presumption that establishes tax residence in Gibraltar.'[317]

We would not be so bold as to state, definitively that 'Gibraltar does not require tax residency to tax an individual's income' but in most cases this will practically be true, and as a result the FAQs lead to the same conclusion that we have arrived at. Namely, that if the treaty is an anti-avoidance treaty, then it should deal predominantly with the concerns of that party whose tax is most likely to be avoided.

316 *Ibid*

317 P18 Frequently Asked Question (FAQs) International Tax Agreement: Gibraltar – Spain issued by HM Government of Gibraltar Income Tax Office in November 2021

Article 2(1)(c) and (d) – Special Rules

'(c) The following special rules for determining residency shall be applied in all cases without prejudice to the criteria set forth in the preceding paragraphs:

(i) Spanish nationals who move their residency to Gibraltar after the date on which this Agreement is signed shall in all cases only be considered tax residents of Spain;

(ii) Non-Spanish nationals who provide proof of their new residency in Gibraltar shall not lose tax residency in Spain. This rule shall apply in the tax period in which the change of residency is made and during the four subsequent tax years. This paragraph shall not apply to non-Spanish nationals that spend less than one complete tax year in Spain or registered Gibraltarians that spend less than 4 years in Spain;

(d) For the purposes of paragraph (1)(c)(ii) above, registered Gibraltarians means any natural person as defined by section 4 of the Gibraltarian Status Act, generally British citizens that have resided in Gibraltar for over ten years;'

Commentary

In Article 2(1)(c) and (d) we can see the strongest echoes of the 1952 Act's ordinarily resident test mirrored for Spanish nationals and Gibraltarians. Art 2(1)(c)(i) is an similar but in reverse of the definition of 'ordinarily resident' in the 1952 Act, and is aimed at similar mischief. All Spanish nationals will be considered tax resident in Spain at all times.

Amongst the profession in Gibraltar there has been some debate as to whether or not this Art (2)(c)(i) applies to those Spanish nationals who move to Gibraltar from some country other than Spain. The FAQs state that:

'Spanish nationals moving their residence from Spain to Gibraltar will retain Spanish tax residency whilst they live in Gibraltar. This has applied since the Treaty was signed on 4 March 2019'.[318]

It is not clear to us that the language of the Tax Treaty supports the assertion that

318 Supra Note 20

Spanish nationals must move from Spain to Gibraltar for the rule to apply, though the context of negotiations may well mean that that was the intention. At the time of writing, we believe this question is yet to be settled and it would require a court case, most likely in the Spanish courts, to settle the application of this rule.

The rules applicable to non-Spanish nationals mirror and extend those which were in force in Spain with regard to Gibraltar and other jurisdictions deemed to be 'non-cooperative' jurisdictions prior to the introduction of the Tax Treaty. They establish a 'tail' of tax residence which continues to adhere to the individual, even when they would otherwise be tax resident in the new jurisdiction. These kinds of anti-avoidance provisions are reasonably common. It is important to note the recognition of 'Registered Gibraltarians' as having a special status and as being subject to less stringent laws than others. It was this to which Fabian Picardo, Chief Minister, referred in his speech to the United Nations on 19th June 2019, when he said:

> 'Spain has now also recognised the existence and legal status of Gibraltarians as distinct from the British generally.'[319]

Article 2(2) – Legal Persons and other legal structures and arrangements

'(2) The following rules for determining tax residency apply:

> (a) Legal persons, entities and other legal structures or arrangements, established and managed in Gibraltar, or governed by its legislation, shall be considered to have residency only in Spain when any of the following circumstances exist:
>
> (i) The majority of the assets, whether directly or indirectly owned, are located in Spain or consist of rights that may or must be exercised in Spain;
>
> (ii) The majority of the income accrued in a calendar year derives from sources in Spain, pursuant to article 13 of the

319 Text of Chief Minister's Address to the United Nations Committee of 24; 18th June 2019

codifying legislation of the Non-resident Income Tax Act of the Spanish tax legislation as may be amended from time to time;

(iii) The majority of the natural persons in charge of effective management are tax resident in Spain;

(iv) The majority of the interests in the capital or equity, voting or profit-sharing rights are under the direct or indirect control of either natural persons who are tax residents in Spain or legal persons, entities and other legal structures or arrangements linked to tax residents in Spain;'

Commentary

It is firstly important to understand that the provisions of Article 2(2) apply not only to legal entities, but to all things which can also be taxpayers or have tax effect. It covers trusts, partnerships, limited liability partnerships and limited partnerships or foundations. It is an article which applies to all things which are legal persons and all things that are not. The only criterion for applicability is that the entity or arrangement in question must be established and managed in Gibraltar or governed by its legislation.

The treatment of unincorporated entities — such as trusts — is not entirely clear. The language itself seems clear: if the unincorporated entity is established and managed in Gibraltar, and it meets the tests below, then it is tax resident in Spain. However, the FAQs seem to deviate from this treatment:

'How do these rules affect structures including other legal arrangements such as trusts?

Spain applies a purposive approach to unincorporated entities.

Their civil law system does not recognise the protection afforded by such legal structures or arrangements that are available under a common law legal system. If a structure contains such legal arrangements, then the impact of these rules will likely need to be considered on the highest corporate or individual layer available, where Spain considers the 'true' purpose, effect, control and ownership to be.

The tax residence of any natural persons at this highest layer would need to

> be established in accordance with the provisions of the Treaty.'[320]

This seems to imply that the Spanish authorities will 'look through' the existence of the trust and tax the person or entity at the top of the ownership chain. If this is then this would seem to make the provisions of Article 2(2) entirely redundant from the perspective of Spanish tax law, in regard to any arrangement without legal personality. Once again, we await the interpretation of the Spanish courts and are left in the meantime simply stating that the position is unclear without judicial guidance. The position taken by the FAQs seems reasonable, but the language of the article states that a legal arrangement managed and established in Gibraltar becomes tax resident in Spain if it meets the relevant criteria.

As to the criteria for tax residence themselves, the form of a tiebreaker has been abandoned in this article and these are simply statements of a corporate tax residence test. The fact that a Gibraltar entity meets the criteria for tax residence in Gibraltar is entirely without relevance for the Tax Treaty and therefore the Tax Treaty diverges from the format of the OECD Model Convention. What happens with the Tax Treaty in effect, is that it creates an addition to the Gibraltar tax residence test contained in s74 of the 2010 Act. Gibraltar now effectively has its original domestic test, in addition to which, where a company or other entity has a relationship with Spain, it is subject to a second domestic test. This is compounded by the fact that Schedule 12 of the 2010 Act now references the Tax Treaty and the provisions of s3B(2) of the 2010 Act state:

> '(2) Where any provision of an International Tax Agreement purports to affect how a tax in Gibraltar is to be charged, determined, calculated, assessed or collected or any matter is to be determined under this Act (a 'Relevant Provision') –
>
> (a) if this Act does not contain a provision dealing with the subject matter of a Relevant Provision, that Relevant Provision shall have direct legal effect as if it were set out in this Act; and
>
> (b) if this Act contains a provision to a contrary or different

320 Supra Note 20

> effect to a Relevant Provision (an 'Existing Provision'), that Relevant Provision shall have direct legal effect by way of modification of the Existing Provision in so far as (but only in so far as) is required to implement or comply with that Relevant Provision in respect of that International Tax Agreement.'

The above effectively incorporates Article 2(2) of the Tax Treaty into Gibraltar statute. The domestic corporate tax residence test is amended by the Tax Treaty, and as a consequence all those provisions which rely on residence (such as the OECD Common Reporting Standard, etc.) are now removed from the Gibraltar Commissioner of Income Tax's remit with regard to such entities. This is an interesting and possibly unforeseen consequence of the Tax Treaty, but one worthy of note.

The tests themselves contained at Article 2(2)(a) are reasonably self-explanatory and can be summed up in the sentence 'a Gibraltar entity is tax resident in Spain if it owns the majority of its assets, makes most of its money in Spain or is managed by or owned by a majority of people located in Spain. This is, of course, a summary; if you believe the Tax Treaty applies to your entity, then detailed advice should be sought.

Article 2(3) - Elimination of double taxation

'(3) The competent authorities shall eliminate, where relevant, double taxation pursuant to the provisions of their domestic law.'

Commentary

This Article 2(3) is the strongest indication that the Tax Treaty is not a double tax treaty in the classical sense. Articles 23A and 23B of the Model Convention give two alternative articles for insertion into a treaty based on the Model Convention. The commentary to the 2017 edition of the Model Convention on these alternative articles runs to 30 pages. Article 2(3) of the Tax Treaty contains 17 words. It is self-explanatory: the parties will simply apply their domestic law and that is that. The treatment of double taxation under the Tax Treaty is no different to that which would have been applied before its introduction.

Article 3. Administrative cooperation in tax matters

'(1) The Parties shall apply an enhanced administrative cooperation with each other, with a view to exchanging information that is foreseeably relevant to the administration, enforcement and collection concerning taxes of all kind and description imposed on behalf of the Parties, their territorial or administrative subdivisions, including local entities.'

Commentary

The Tax Treaty commits both jurisdictions to an enhanced cooperation programme, which is designed to at least replace the provisions of EU cooperation which have been lost due to Brexit, but also to extend cooperation to some practical provisions. In qualifying that the enhanced administrative cooperation is sought only with a view to exchanging 'foreseeably relevant' information, a notional safeguard is provided to the taxpayer who is, in consequence, only obliged to provide such information as satisfies that criterion of relevance. However, the authors have serious doubt as to whether or not this safeguard retains any efficacy when compared to the prescribed list of information to be exchanged, all of which is, presumably, deemed 'foreseeably relevant' and will therefore be exchanged, whether relevant or not.

The remainder of Article 3 is extensive and we will not seek to analyse each provision. However, we will highlight those which we feel are of note.

> 'Art 3(2) – Article 3(2) commits parties to implement with regard to each other, post Brexit, a number of provisions of equivalent effect to European Union legislation with regard to mutual administrative assistance. In particular information exchange and mutual recovery and the Council of Europe's Multilateral Convention on Mutual Administrative Assistance in Tax Matters.[321]

It is fair to say that much of this was already in place (one exception being DAC6 which has now been implemented by Gibraltar in regard to matters which regard Spain) and is simply a maintenance of the status quo.

321 p218 Brown, H and Jackson, G, 'A Practitioners Guide to Tax Information Exchange Regimes', Spiramus 2021

'Art 3(5) – the Gibraltarian authorities will furnish information on:

i. Workers registered in Gibraltar who are resident in Spain;
ii. Six monthly information on vessels, aircraft and motor vehicles registered in Gibraltar relating to tax residents in Spain;
iii. Direct and free access to the Register of Companies
iv. Direct access to the beneficial ownership register
v. Direct access to information available to the Commissioner of Income Tax on trust or similar related matters'

From an academic perspective, these are robust and novel provisions, since direct and free access is a broader conception of cooperation than is normally seen. The authors are not privy to what systems have been put in place since the introduction of the Tax Treaty, though they must amount to unfettered access for the Spanish authorities.

'Art 3(10) – The Spanish authorities will furnish information on:

i. Annual information on workers in Spain who are resident in Gibraltar[322]
ii. Six-monthly information on vessels, aircraft, and motor vehicles newly registered in Spain relating to Gibraltar.'

Of five obligations, only two are mirrored by Spain. In the second of those two, the Spanish obligation is limited to newly registered vehicles, whereas Gibraltar must file information on all such vehicles, new or otherwise.

Article 6. Information exchange, Confidentiality and Data Safeguards

'Information exchanged under this Agreement is subject to the rules provided in Articles 21 and 22 of the Convention on Mutual Administrative Assistance in Tax Matters of the OECD and the Council of Europe.'

322 this section is in identical language to Art 3(5)(a) which imposes the reciprocal burden on Gibraltar

Commentary

Article 6 does give some comfort, in that the data processing provisions of the Model Convention are applicable to the information exchanged under this Tax Treaty.

The Tax Treaty in International Context

The authors believe that the Tax treaty will remain a unique document for the foreseeable future. Comparisons have been made with the Franco-Monégasque tax treaty of 1963[323]. This is, in itself, worthy of consideration. Sitting as Monaco does, in a relationship to its larger neighbour geographically similar to that of Gibraltar to Spain, it is tempting to draw analogies between the two. However, there are some key differences, not least of which is that France does not dispute Monaco's existence; in fact it has recognised the principality's independence since 1511.[324] France and Monaco also have a history of functioning tax treaties, the first in 1951 and the second in 1963.

Similarities between the France/Monaco relationship and the Spain/Gibraltar relationship should not be overplayed:

> Since by land Monaco is entirely surrounded by France, its independence clearly depends on French protection. Its foreign policy is controlled by France, and economically it has been part of France by a succession of customs unions.[325]

Not all of these factors are relevant to Spain, though to a certain extent an element of Spanish consent to Gibraltar's existence must subsist given its geographical relation. Neither do the factors in the quote map well on to the Gibraltar-UK relationship. Furthermore, while the 2019 Tax Treaty can be seen as a pre-emptive

323 HM Government of Gibraltar Press Release 165/2021 Chief Minister's Note on Parliamentary Resolution for the Introduction of Gazette Notice to Implement Tax Treaty with Spain, 26th February 2021

324 P663 J. K. Nolan and G. S. Blair, 'Business in Monaco Under the New Treaty with France', *The Business Lawyer* April 1964

325 *Ibid* p664

measure to avoid future confrontations between the two parties, post-Brexit, the 1963 Franco-Monégasque Treaty was a response to an unfolding crisis, as clashing interests threatened stability. The Tax Treaty was not born out of unfolding crisis. The Franco-Monégasque Treaty came about only after the suspension of traffic into Monaco; following this, the lapsing of the customs union and of related treaties between the two, and substantial pressure from France, Monaco conceded the point and signed the 1963 Treaty.[326] No events as dramatic as these occurred during the negotiations of three willing participants which gave rise to the Tax Treaty of 2019, although clearly UK withdrawal from the European Union was the trigger

The most striking similarity between the Franco-Monégasque Treaty of 1963 and Gibraltar's 2019 Tax Treaty is to be found in Article 7 of the former. Article 7 of the 1963 Treaty provides for French nationals resident in Monaco to be subject to French income tax on their global income, as if they were resident in France, unless they had been residing in Monaco for five years on 13th October 1962. In other words, it is an effective mirror of Article 2(1)(c)(i) of the Tax Treaty; for a person of French nationality moving to Monaco after a given date (i.e. 13th October 1957), the Monégasque tax regime has no impact. Similarly, for a Spanish national relocating to Gibraltar after 4th May 2019, the effect of the Gibraltar tax regime is entirely neutralised on a personal level, by virtue of his continued residence in Spain.

There are clear similarities between the 1963 Treaty and the Tax Treaty; however, there are also noteworthy divergences. The 1963 Treaty imposes a corporate tax rate (applicable in certain circumstances) which is linked to the French rate,[327] but the Tax Treaty does not go so far. They are not entirely analogous as documents, but they are similar in their effects. Despite the differences in the relationships between France and Monaco and between Spain and Gibraltar, and the fact that the 1963 Treaty was borne out of a direct confrontation rather than the threat of one occurring in the future, both treaties can usefully be described as anti-avoidance treaties. Further research on the parallels between the texts and the practical application of both treaties would be welcomed by the authors.

---

326 *Ibid* p666

327 Article 1

Conclusion

Gibraltar cannot deny the existence of Spain, and we believe we have shown that, in terms of its taxation system, it never has. Whether it was adapting an Empire-wide model to its own specific geographic peculiarities, or in latter years understanding the need to be a good neighbour and work in the context of its position as a member of a community of Iberian jurisdictions — however fractious that community might become at times — it has acknowledged the existence of Spain and the innately cross-border character of both its workforce and its population.

The coming years will present further challenge; these will best be met by understanding that these facts of geography have not changed, and never will.

Chapter 8

YOU'RE NOT IN THE UK NOW

The principle of a distinct jurisdiction: The EU and the development of Gibraltar Law as a thing unto itself

Grahame Jackson and Isaac Levy

Introduction

The constitutional relationships between the UK and Gibraltar, and Gibraltar and the EU, are and were complex and not without their difficulties. For the purposes of this chapter, we will assume that the relationship between Gibraltar and the UK is settled and that the UK recognises Gibraltar as an entirely separate jurisdiction. The outstanding legal text on the position is British Overseas Territories Law by Hendry and Dickson[328] which deals with the legal and constitutional framework on a technical level. From a less technical perspective, there are many strong pieces from across the divide including Gibraltar: 'The Making of a People'[329] by the current Deputy Chief Minister Dr Joseph Garcia.

The matter which is at hand in this Chapter is not whether the United Kingdom recognises that Gibraltar is a separate jurisdiction, but instead that the world outside that relationship does so and that the jurisdiction is "real" as a result. The recognition of units which have been devolved out of another state is a matter of politics and diplomacy. States and territories born out of other states or territories do not in any real context "exist" until they are acknowledged by the international community. This applies to all those states which are born of others through whichever route they choose. A unilateral declaration of independence which could be seen as an act of self-determination is ineffective until accepted by the international community; that consent from the outside world converts

328 Hendry I and Dickinson, S British Overseas Territory Law, Hart Publishing 2018

329 Garcia, J, Gibraltar: The Making of a People, Panorama Publishing, 1994

"rebels" into a legitimate government representing a people.[330] Similarly, the granting of "independence" by one state to a region of its territory must also be recognised by the international community.[331]

It is, therefore, of interest to us that there has been a process by which an international organisation has acknowledged the right of Gibraltar to have to itself a separate taxing authority from that of the UK. That organisation was the European Union (the EU) and, in this chapter, we will discuss the narrative of the relations between Gibraltar and the EU, the various cases and principles in play.

Gibraltar's status in the EU.

As of 1st February 2020, the United Kingdom left the EU taking with it a reluctant Gibraltar. Gibraltar had become an EU territory (then the European Economic Community) on 1st January 1973 and had occupied a unique position as a "territory for whose external relations a Member State is responsible", [332] as such the Treaties which make up the 'constitution' of the European Union were applicable in their totality to Gibraltar (though such matters as the Schengen travel zone and monetary union were also not applicable to Gibraltar by virtue of Article 28 of the UK's Act of Accession to the EEC). This unique status meant that the UK was responsible before the EU for the implementation of European law in Gibraltar, and action to enforce compliance with such law was taken against the United Kingdom rather than Gibraltar itself.[333] In other words, in a sense, Gibraltar had

330 The examples of this are too numerous to mention, though the Biafra conflict is a good example of a failed attempt to establish a state

331 One strong example of this is the case of what were known as the "Bantustans" in the territory of South Africa, unrecognised statelets which formed part of the Apartheid system.

332 At the time Article 227(4) EEC Treaty and now Article 355(3) Treaty on the Functioning of the European Union

333 This particular arrangement, that a devolved government of Gibraltar was the entity which would implement various laws mandated by the EU whilst it was the UK which would suffer enforcement if those laws were not implemented, is one of the arguments made in favour of the retention of such provisions as the Royal Prerogative powers of the Crown in relation to Gibraltar or the power of the Westminster Parlia-

no standing before the EU, whilst it was recognised as a separate territory under the responsibility of a Member State. It is this that explains why the various cases we will discuss below were actions against the United Kingdom as a party rather than, or in addition to, Gibraltar itself.

EU Scrutiny and the long road to recognition of the Gibraltarian taxation system.

Beginning in 1998, with the OECD's Report Harmful Tax Competition: An Emerging Global Issue[334]which had recommended that OECD Member States "refrain, review and remove"[335] where harmful tax practices were concerned, the EU began to actively consider the position of 'harmful tax practices' within the Union. There were a number of territories and Member States which had regimes which would be considered, and Gibraltar is certainly not isolated in its position as a territory which has come under scrutiny.

The methods by which the EU mounts its scrutiny are twofold.

Given the fact that direct taxation is not within the remit of the European Union, but is instead the remit of the Member States, there are limited tools which the EU can utilise to enforce the abolition of 'harmful tax practices'. The Commission and Ministers of Finance were obviously cognizant of this limitation when they established the first pillar of the EU's internal mechanisms to eradicate 'harmful tax practices' within the Union. That is the Code of Conduct Group (Business Taxation)[336], established in 1997-a group which does not have formal enforcement powers but instead carries a political weight when it reports in connection with Member States and their tax affairs.

The only formal method by which the EU can force a Member State (in this

---

ment to legislate directly for Gibraltar without reference to the Gibraltar Parliament. For a broader discussion of the powers of the UK in relation to Gibraltar see Hendry I and Dickinson, S British Overseas Territory Law, Hart Publishing 2018.

334 *Harmful Tax Competition: An Emerging Global Issue,* OECD Publishing [1998]

335 Weiner, JM, Ault HJ, 'The OECD's Report on Harmful Tax Competition', National Tax Journal, Volume 1 No 3 [1998]

336 Please see further: https://www.consilium.europa.eu/en/council-eu/preparatory-bodies/code-conduct-group/ (Last accessed on 26th February 2024).

case the United Kingdom on behalf of the Government of Gibraltar) to comply with Union-wide law related to tax is through the deployment of their powers under Article 107 of the Treaty on the Functioning of the European Union (TFEU), which states;

> Save as otherwise provided in the Treaties, any aid granted by a Member State or through State resources in any form whatsoever which distorts or threatens to distort competition by favouring certain undertakings or the production of certain goods shall, in so far as it affects trade between Member States, be incompatible with the internal market.[337]

State Aid is divided into two broad categories;

i. Existing aid is aid which was in place either before the establishment of the predecessor to the EU in 1958, or the accession of the relevant member state. In terms of Gibraltar the relevant date is 1st January 1973. Such existing aid is to be monitored by the Commission under art 108(1) of TFEU;
ii. New Aid is aid which is introduced after accession.

Existing aid is deemed to be lawful State Aid, in the case of New Aid it is deemed unlawful unless the procedure contained in Art 108(3) of TFEU is followed and the Commission approves of the aid in question. We will revisit this distinction below.

Throughout the period in question (from 1998 to 2021) it is these two mechanisms which have been deployed when analysing the Gibraltar taxation system.

2001 State Aid Investigation into exempt and qualifying companies

On 12th February 1999, as part of a wider action against 'harmful tax practices' the Commission opened an investigation into five Gibraltar "schemes" by requesting information from the UK as to their operation. After consideration

337 The now Article 107(1) Treaty on the Functioning of the European Union.

on 11th July 2001, the European Commission issued its decision to initiate the formal investigation procedure under the State Aid Rules in TFEU on not only the Gibraltar schemes, but also a number of other schemes in multiple Member States.[338] Of the 15 schemes judged to be harmful, two were related to Gibraltar:

i. Qualifying Offshore Companies incorporated under the combined effects of the Income Tax (Amendment) Ordinance 1983 and the Income Tax (Qualifying Companies) Rules 1984. Qualifying Companies under this scheme were taxed at a rate "to be prescribed" which must have been no less than 2% and no more than 35%.[339]
ii. Exempt Companies. Which was a company which was approved to be exempt from taxation under the Taxation (Concessions and Exemptions) Ordinance 1967.

The case came before the Court of First Instance of the European Union on 5th March 2002, with judgment handed down on 30th April 2002.[340] In that judgment, it was confirmed that the Qualifying Company regime, which was instituted after

338 See Commission press release of 11 July 2001, in: IP/01/982. The procedures concerned the following harmful schemes, respectively: 1. the German Coordination Centres scheme; 2. the Spanish Biscaye Province Co-ordination Centres; 3. the French Headquarters and Logistics Centres scheme; 4. the Irish Foreign Income scheme; the schemes for 5. Luxembourg's Coordination Centres and 6. Luxembourg's Finance Companies; 7. the Netherlands' International Financial Activities scheme; 8. the Finnish Åland Islands' Captive Insurance scheme; 9. the UK's Gibraltar Qualifying Offshore Companies; and 10. Gibraltar Exempt Offshore Companies; 11. the Belgian Coordination Centres scheme; 12 Greek Foreign Companies Offices scheme; and 13. Italy's Trieste's Financial and Insurance Centres scheme; as well as the following two non-harmful measures: 14. the French Central Corporate Treasuries scheme; and 15. the Swedish Foreign Insurance Companies scheme.

339 This regime is still listed in regulation 3 of the UK's Controlled Foreign Companies (Designer Rate Tax Provisions) Regulations 2000 as a "Specified Designer Rate Tax Provision"

340 Available online on: Joined Cases T-195/01 and T-207/01, *Government of Gibraltar v European Commission*. https://eur-lex.europa.eu/legal-content/EN/TXT/PDF/?uri=CELEX:62001TJ0195&from=EN (Last accessed on 26th February 2024)

the United Kingdom and Gibraltar became part of the then European Community, amounted to "new" aid (and therefore, had to be immediately ceased) and the Exempt Company Regime, which was instituted before the United Kingdom and Gibraltar acceded to the EU treaties, was "pre-existing" aid and was therefore legal.[341]

It is important to note that the victory of the Commission in regard to Qualifying Companies could well have led to the issuance of a Recovery Notice under the State Aid procedure, which would have forced the Gibraltar Government to recover the "aid" it had granted to Qualifying Companies, that being the difference between 35% standard corporate tax rate and the 2% - 10% rate commonly paid by Qualifying Companies. The published record does not appear to reflect the reasons for the European Commission's decision not to order recovery, though the authors would speculate that amongst the influences on that decision was the Government of Gibraltar's willingness to embrace a reform which would resolve the issue as a whole including the Exempt Company Regime as well as the relatively novel approach by the European Commission to use state aid rules to tackle entire regimes of corporate taxation. The Gibraltar Government announced on 27th April 2002 its intention to repeal all laws in connection with the taxation of companies and introduce an entirely new regime. This intention was confirmed by the UK in its letter of 12th August 2002 to the Commission when it formally notified the new regime to the Commission for clearance under state aid rules.

The aim of the Government of Gibraltar in reforming the Income Tax system as a whole at this point was:

> To create a completely different form of tax regime which, while offering advantages to companies with no activities in Gibraltar, would not be achieving its aim by discriminatory taxes.[342]

This led to a never implemented yet important (for our purposes) proposal, the Gibraltar 'Employment Tax'.

---

341 This decision was despite the fact that the Exempt Company Regime had undergone slight legislative reform in 1983, the court considered that those changes were insufficient to mean that the amended regime was "new aid".

342 Grahame Jackson, 'From Outcast to Acceptance' (unpublished), (2020) p.30

Employment Tax – an important dead end.

The proposal, which was submitted by the UK government on behalf of Gibraltar on the 12th August 2002, was made up of a charge to taxation applicable to all companies in Gibraltar, with a "top up" applicable to Financial Services entities and utilities companies. We shall call this proposal in the round "the Employment Tax Proposal".[343]

The main part of the tax charge would be made up of three charges:

i. A payroll tax of £3000 per employee
ii. A Business Property Occupation Tax related to the rateable value of the property occupied by the business
iii. A Registration Fee of £150 or £300 depending on whether or not the company was intended to generate income.

It is true that this proposed arrangement would have been entirely novel amongst developed jurisdictions, and there is a slight whiff of a proposal designed 'by committee' rather than an intellectually coherent whole. As Sir Peter Caruana himself stated;

> it had the look of an exception in the European Union and would not have been sustainable today. It would have been the only system of its kind in the world and subject to constant scrutiny as such. We retreated from it as plausible during the early stages of the Commission's investigation.[344]

The exact details of the proposal which was so swiftly dropped are not entirely important for our purposes, however, the importance of the Employment Tax proposal is not in its details, but in the response which it triggered.

On 16th October 2002, the EC Commission notified the UK of its intention to investigate utilising its powers under the State Aid provisions. On 30th March 2004, the Commission gave its decision that the reform proposal amounted to

343 See Joined Cases T-211/04 and T-215/04, *Government of Gibraltar (T-211/04) and United Kingdom (T-215/04) v European Commission*. Paragraph 18

344 Grahame Jackson, 'From Outcast to Acceptance' (unpublished), (2020) p.32

state aid. That decision stated:

> the notified measures therefore entail both a regional and a material selectivity and the latter follows both from a number of specific features of the proposed system and from the analysis of that system as a whole.[345]

It is worthy of note that the European justice system worked so slowly that the employment tax proposal had been jettisoned long before anything approaching a decision had been given. Despite this, the findings of the Court of Justice of the European Union (CJEU) when the matter was finally settled are vitally important in the recognition of the Gibraltar taxation system as distinct from the UK system, and that the jurisdiction of Gibraltar as a taxing authority exists.

As discussed above, the EC Commission found that the Employment Tax Proposal was both materially and regionally selective. It is worth, therefore, considering what these terms (regional, material and selective) mean and why they are important.

Selectivity in general

Selectivity is that a distinction is made between sectors, or regions, or undertakings within an economy (i.e. the provision in question is "selectively" applied). In relation to taxation, the method by which a target is "selected" is that there is a derogation from a "system of reference" (that is the standard regime of taxation).

Material Selectivity

Material Selectivity is defined by the Commission as:

> The material selectivity of a measure implies that the measure applies only to certain (groups of) undertakings or certain sectors of the economy in a given Member State.[346]

Therefore, in order to be materially selective a measure must apply only to certain identifiable groups or undertakings. So, we can imagine a provision which

345 Recital 152 Decision 2005/261/EC

346 Commission Notice on the notion of State aid as referred to in Article 107(1) of the Treaty on the Functioning of the European Union (2016/C 262/01)

subsidises car manufacturers by lowering their tax rate to zero, that would be materially selective.

Regional Selectivity

Regional Selectivity arises where a provision is applicable only in a given region of a Member State, and that that regionally applicable provision gives rise to an advantage to that region.

However, there are situations under which a provision which may appear to be regionally selective. As shown in what is now known as the *Azores*[347] case, the CJEU is willing to recognise the devolved powers of a territory within a Member State in given circumstances, and respect the policy decisions of the separate administrative jurisdiction within the Member State, even if they would otherwise grant a regionally selective advantage. It does this by acknowledging that, in certain circumstances, the "system of reference" need not be the overarching system of the Member State.

The *Azores* case lays down a three-part test which permits the "system of reference" to be that which is utilised at the regional level and not the overall system of the Member State but that of the region itself:

i. Institutional Autonomy:

The Commission Notice on the notion of State Aid states:

> The existence of institutional autonomy can be established where the tax measure decision has been taken by a regional or local authority with its own constitutional, political and administrative status that is separate from that of the central government.[348]
>
> It is clear to anyone who has a constitutional understanding of Gibraltar that this criteria is met in the circumstances of Gibraltar.

ii. Procedural Autonomy

Similarly, the Commission Notice states the following in regard to Procedural Autonomy:

---

347 *Portugal v Commission*, C-88/03, ECLI:EU:C:2006:511,

348 Commission Notice on the notion of State aid as referred to in Article 107(1) of the Treaty on the Functioning of the European Union (2016/C 262/01) para 145

> The existence of procedural autonomy can be established where a tax measure decision has been adopted without the central government being able to directly intervene in determining its content.[349]
>
> This procedural autonomy is clear from the Gibraltar Constitution Order Article 32 "Power to Make Laws".

iii. Financial Autonomy

Finally, there is a requirement for Financial Autonomy:

> The existence of economic and financial autonomy can be established where an infra-State body assumes responsibility for the political and financial consequences of a tax reduction measure. This cannot be the case if the infra-State body is not responsible for managing a budget, that is to say when it does not have control of both revenue and expenditure.[350]

Gibraltar is responsible for its own financial affairs and has a budget entirely separate from the UK.

The decision of the General Court in December of 2008 ruled that Gibraltar did meet the criteria in the *Azores* case and therefore, the Employment Tax Proposal was not Regionally Selective. The Commission and the Kingdom of Spain then mounted a further appeal which was not resolved until 2011. The final decision in the long running case around the selectivity or otherwise of the Employment Tax Proposal was handed down on 15th April 2011. Whilst the question of Material Selectivity was resolved against the position of the Gibraltar Government, the court did not review the position of the General Court on the question of Regional Selectivity thus leaving in place its decision that Gibraltar met the Azores criteria,[351] and that the correct Reference System to apply when considering the Gibraltar taxation provisions was NOT the UK's system, but the underlying Gibraltar taxation system. In other words, Gibraltar was acknowledged as a separate taxing

349 Commission Notice on the notion of State aid as referred to in Article 107(1) of the Treaty on the Functioning of the European Union (2016/C 262/01) para 147

350 Commission Notice on the notion of State aid as referred to in Article 107(1) of the Treaty on the Functioning of the European Union (2016/C 262/01) para 152

351 Government of Gibraltar Press Release ref: 339/2011

authority with a unique system which exists as distinct from the UK.

Further Challenges

The phasing out of the Exempt Company regime which Gibraltar had committed to before the Employment Tax Proposal was finally completed on 31st December 2010, a date that coincided with the introduction of a new Income Tax Act which (for the most part) simply recodified and renewed the 1952 Income Tax Act.

The only major change which is of note between the Income Tax Act 2010 and the Income Tax Act 1952 was the abolition of the charge to tax on interest and royalties. Both of these provisions were subject to the territorial principle in the 1952 Act, and given the uncertainty of case law in the United Kingdom (for example the multi-factoral test described in *National Bank of Greece*[352]) the charges had become rather moribund. As a result, there was strong lobbying to remove the charges all together and so there was no charge to tax on interest or royalties in the Income Tax Act 2010 as first enacted.[353] It could be argued that this was an error, and a closer recodification of the 1952 Act would have been a less risky approach. However, that is not what occurred, and the events which followed were to a certain extent a confirmation of Gibraltar's position, despite their negative outcome.

On 1st June 2012, the Spanish Government issued a complaint to the EU Commission that the removal of the charges to tax on interest and royalties amounted to new aid, and was thus illegal under the State Aid provisions. In addition, they renewed their claim that Gibraltar having a separate taxation system was inevitably regionally selective.

To a certain extent, the Spanish complaint was almost already redundant. The EU Code of Conduct Group (see above) had already raised the issue and the Gibraltar Government had engaged in order to resolve the matter. Within a year, and before the Commission had made any decision as whether or not to investigate the Spanish complaint, the Class 1A and Class 3 charges on companies in receipt of inter-company interest and royalties (respectively) had been introduced. The

352 *National Bank of Greece SA v Westminster Bank Executor & Trustee Co* (Channel Islands) [1971] A.C. 945 (11 November 1970)

353 Grahame Jackson, 'From Outcast to Acceptance' (unpublished), (2020) p.57

language of the new charges was more robust than the 1952 versions, and therefore more certain in their applicability.

In addition, in their October 2013 decision to investigate the 1st June 2012 complaint, the EU Commission rejected the claim of regional selectivity that the Spanish had made:

> In this context, the reference framework corresponds exclusively to the geographical limits of the territory of Gibraltar and so no regional selectivity can be identified on the ground that the tax regime applies to Gibraltar only.[354]

Therefore, the Spanish line of attack that Gibraltar is merely a region of the UK which cannot be acknowledged as a separate jurisdiction (similar lines of policy can be seen across the board in Spain's dealings with Gibraltar) was closed. The Government of Gibraltar was, understandably, delighted, as the Chief Minister, Fabian Picardo said:

> What is significant today is that the Commission has accepted the territoriality system as the system of reference, it has confirmed that the 2013 amendment addresses its concerns regarding interest and made a robust statement on regional selectivity. This is very good news for Gibraltar.[355]

The scrutiny of the Gibraltar taxation system (just as with all the other systems in the EU) did not end in 2013. On 1st October 2014, the EU expanded its investigation to cover the possibility that State Aid was being granted via the issuance of "tax rulings"[356] and found 5 out of 165 considered rulings did amount to State Aid. It also found that the removal of the charge to interest in the 2010 Act amounted to State Aid, which had already been resolved by the 2013 amendment of the Income Tax Act 2010 to include the Class 1A Charge on inter-company interest. None of these findings related to regionality but instead procedural issues, which have been resolved by the authorities by the introduction of a statutory regime for rulings at Part 1A of the Income Tax Act 2010. These decisions were made in the

354 EU Commission Letter to UK State aid SA.34914 (2013/C) - (ex 2013/NN) – United Kingdom Gibraltar corporate tax regime. Para 58

355 Government of Gibraltar Press Release 732/2013

356 ec.europa.eu/commission/presscorner/detail/en/IP_14_1073

Commission Decision of 19th December 2018.[357]

Never one to be deterred by failure, the Spanish authorities mounted one more attempt to force regional selectivity before the courts of the European Union when they appealed against the EU Commission's decision of 19th December 2018 on the grounds that it denied regional selectivity as a ground for considering matters of State Aid.

As a final step in this long running saga, in the run up to the exit of the United Kingdom and Gibraltar from the European Union, Spain dropped its case on 20th December 2020, 12 days before British exit from the EU. The case was still vitally important to the Gibraltarian position that it is more than simply an appendage of the UK. As the Chief Minister, Fabian Picardo said;

> perhaps more importantly, we will now leave the EU with clarity that on such a fundamental issue as Gibraltar's independent taxing powers there was never a requirement that Gibraltar should be treated as part of the UK's fiscal territory.[358]

Conclusion

Gibraltar fought for, and won, the right to be considered a separate jurisdiction within the EU. It is true that, were it not for the *Azores* case, then the requirement for Gibraltar to align with the UK or suffer accusations of Regional Selectivity would have had to have been examined in unchartered territory even though the Gibraltar case was solid, not least, as a result of the old age adage of "No taxation without representation" (a ridiculous consequence of applying the concept of regional selectivity to the UK-Gibraltar constitutional relationship since the people of Gibraltar do not have the right to vote in elections to the Westminster Parliament). But the *Azores* case reached the CJEU first and provided the test to be applied. It is logical that the application of principles established in a

357 Commission Decision (EU) 2019/700 of 19 December 2018 on the State Aid SA.34914 (2013/C) implemented by the United Kingdom as regards the Gibraltar Corporate Income Tax Regime.

358 'Spanish Government drops legal challenge to Gibraltar's fiscal independence', Gibraltar Chronicle 23rd December 2023.

less politically charged context than that of Gibraltar and Spain is easier than establishing those principles directly. Ultimately, it was a victory for Gibraltar as it established that an organisation, of which Spain is a part, was obliged to recognise laws in Gibraltar – made by Gibraltarians – as separate from those of the UK and subject to an exercise of sovereignty by the Gibraltar Parliament and not by the Westminster Parliament.

The wider stage…an emerging jurisdiction…a change in form

The general principle which underlies the entry into international agreements by Gibraltar is that if the agreement is a treaty between sovereign states, then Gibraltar cannot be a party to a treaty as it is not a sovereign state.[359] This is the position of the UK and one to which Gibraltar has adhered. Where a Gibraltarian does sign an international agreement then he does so under powers granted to him by Letters of Entrustment granted by the UK. This was the case when the then Chief Minister, Sir Peter Caruana, entered into a Tax Information Exchange Agreement with the United States.

The opposite extreme of a Gibraltarian acting under a Letter of Entrustment can be seen in the arrangements regarding the OECD and Council of Europe Convention on Mutual Administrative Assistance on Tax Matters (the Convention). The United Kingdom entered into the Convention in 2007, but Gibraltar was unable to enter directly into the Convention due to its status as an overseas territory. It was only on 1st March 2014 that the Convention came into force for Gibraltar as a result of an extension request issued by the United Kingdom in December 2013. It is true that the UK would not have extended the Convention to Gibraltar without a request and consent from Gibraltar, but it is worthy of note that the form of the arrangement was devoid of any recognition of Gibraltar as a party to the Convention, even though it imposes obligations on Gibraltar.

---

359 There is some debate as to the meaning of the word "state" and under some interpretations Gibraltar could well qualify as a state. See Jackson, Grahame, 'Understanding the Beps and Other OECD Tax Initiatives Including the Inclusive Framework in the Context of Treaties and State Inequality' (July 6, 2023). Journal of Tax Administration, Forthcoming , Available at SSRN: https://ssrn.com/abstract=4502101 (Last accessed on 26th February 2024)

This form of states entering into treaties to engage in cooperation is less commonly utilised in 2023 than it was in 2007. The main method of ensuring cooperation today is not by a formal treaty, but by a "Competent Authority Agreement" between the authorities of the various jurisdictions. It is by this mechanism that Gibraltar can enter into the Multilateral Competent Authority Agreement for on Automatic Exchange of Financial Account Information (CRS), or can be a member of the OECD Inclusive Framework on Base Erosion and Profit Shifting (IF). [360] These fora and agreements are between taxing authorities and not between states. Thus, all the British Overseas Territories which have materially large economies are part of the Inclusive Framework and are acknowledged as distinct jurisdictions in their own right.

This may well smart for the constitutional purist, however, it is entirely logical. The move to encourage cooperation must be one based on consent. One cannot insist on compliance from a recalcitrant jurisdiction with no representation in the relevant fora. From a self-determination perspective, these developments should only be welcomed. Gibraltar is growing as a jurisdiction. Its economy is an equivalent size to that of much larger jurisdictions, and as such it should be recognised as a party to many of these agreements.

The authors, though, would strike a note of caution. The United Nations has recently attempted to seize control of the international tax reform process[361]. If it succeeds, then there is a risk that the reform process will cease to be the business of the widely drawn (though imperfect) IF, and will instead be solely the business of the member states of the United Nations. This would amount to a retrograde step from the perspective of Gibraltar. Much has been written about the imperfections

---

360 Once again one can see the results of the territorial dispute which Gibraltar is subject to. Spain consistently blocked the inclusion of Gibraltar in the IF for the very reason that Gibraltar would be recognised separately by the IF. It is only by the introduction of the Spanish Tax Treaty that the Spanish veto on Gibraltarian membership of the IF was withdrawn. See. "Gibraltar Joins the OECD Inclusive Framework on Base Erosion and Profit Shifting as a Full Members" HM Govt of Gibraltar Press Release 521/2019

361 Please see further: UN Vote Challenges OECD global tax leadership, Thomas, L. Reuters https://www.reuters.com/world/un-vote-challenges-oecd-global-tax-leadership-2023-11-23/ (Last accessed on 26th February 2024)

of the IF,[362] but the broad-based membership of jurisdictions and not "states" gives it a legitimacy which a UN based body with a limited membership criteria would not have.

Conclusion

Since the turn of the millennium, Gibraltar has grown on the international stage. It is recognised as more than a simple adjunct to the United Kingdom, and its authorities now sit as equals with those of sovereign states in broad based fora. This is a function of two things. First,the realisation of the global community that jurisdictions like Gibraltar exist and have rights (as per the EU decisions), and that their cooperation is required to deliver the desired reform agenda post 2000. Second, the increased levels of competence and understanding that Gibraltar and similar jurisdictions have of themselves in the world means that they are open to such cooperation and willing to stand as jurisdictions distinct from their "mother country".

The authors are sure that Gibraltar will continue to embrace its self determination and its participation as an equal on a global tax stage is a vital element of that development.

362 See de la Feria, Rita, 'The Perceived (Un)Fairness of the Global Minimum Corporate Tax Rate' (October 30, 2023). In W. Haslehner et al (eds), The Pillar 2 Global Minimum Tax (Edward Elgar, 2023), forthcoming, Available at SSRN: https://ssrn.com/abstract=4205720 for a useful summary (Last accessed on 26th February 2024)

THE CONTRIBUTORS

Isaac Levy

Isaac is a corporate law and tax specialist with a focus on both corporate and private client transactional and structuring work. Isaac's work with global finance institutions and international real estate groups alike, stems from his highly regarded expertise in tax and his recognised leadership/project management in international corporate transactional and tax work. Recognised by Chambers and Partners as a leading lawyer in its Global and Europe editions, Isaac has been described in the following manner; 'He is a fast thinker, has a sharp mind and is quick to spot the challenges and come up with solutions'- Chambers Global

In the tax context, Isaac has acted for and advised, amongst others, Her Majesty's Government of Gibraltar ('HMGoG'), in respect of amendments to, and transposition of, tax legislation. He has advised HMGoG in respect of the international exchange of tax information and double tax treaties. He formed part of the team that advised HMGoG in respect of the EU Commission state aid investigation. He also drafted the Guidance issued by the Income Tax Office in respect of the accrued and derived principle and tax rulings procedure. Isaac has lectured on Gibraltar tax law at the University of Gibraltar since 2017.

Grahame Jackson ADIT CTA (Fellow)

Grahame is a partner with Hassans International Law Firm in Gibraltar. He has a keen interest in writing about tax and has been published in a number of journals including Intertax, the Journal of Tax Administration and the Bulletin for International Taxation. His academic work focuses on the development of small jurisdictions and sovereignty in relation to international tax reform, international exchange of information and Gibraltar-related issues. Professionally he focuses on international cross border taxation, relocations, corporate taxation and international tax reform.

Grahame is a solicitor in England and Wales and Gibraltar, he qualified late in life in 2008, having previously worked as a printer, a company secretary and a paralegal. He completed the Chartered Institute of Taxation's Advanced Diploma in International Taxation in 2020, he was awarded Fellowship of the Chartered

Institute of Taxation in 2023.

He is also co-presenter of tax podcast 'International Tax Bites' with Harriet Brown of Old Square Tax Chambers which has listeners in over 120 countries, chairman of the Gibraltar Association of Tax Advisers and a member of the panel of judges for the Biennial Gibraltar Tax Essay Prize. He is the co-author of A Practitioner's Guide to International Tax Information Exchange Regimes (Spiramus Press, 2020).

He has lived in Gibraltar since 2002 and has four children, two dogs and a cat.

Thomas Blagden

Thomas is a junior associate in Hassans International Law Firm's Corporate and Commercial Department in Gibraltar. His practice focuses primarily on property finance (including development finance), acquisition finance, cross-border finance, corporate restructures, and private client work.

He joined the firm in 2020 before qualifying into the Corporate and Commercial department in 2022. He is a solicitor admitted to practice in Gibraltar, England and Wales.

Thomas studied Law with European Law (LLB) at the University of Nottingham, spending a year studying Spanish Law at the Universidad Complutense de Madrid, before completing the LPC at BPP University London Holborn.

Outside of work, Thomas is an avid skier and sailor, representing Gibraltar internationally in the latter.

Brian Caetano

Brian is a trainee barrister who started working in Hassans in 2022 after having completed his studies in the UK and The Netherlands. Initially Brian studied Philosophy, Politics and Economics, followed by a Masters in Political Science with a specialisation in EU policy.

Following this and prior to commencing his career in Hassans, Brian undertook an LLB, LLM and the Bar.

Brian has a keen interest in commercial affairs and Gibraltar tax. He has been able to work on a number of matters within these fields, with a greater focus on the area of corporate taxation.

Brian is very interested in local politics and policy making. His hobbies are football and boxing.

Tania Rahmany

Tania is a Senior Associate in Hassans' Corporate and Commercial Department, having joined the firm in 2015. Tania has gained experience in transactional work involving Gibraltar-based structures, largely for UK and European commercial investments. Tania also advises on corporate restructuring, mergers and acquisitions, joint ventures, flotations of companies on recognised stock exchanges, and the incorporation and uses of Gibraltar foundations, and can assist with the Gibraltar tax aspects of any such transaction. Tania is also frequently sought out for tax advisory work, and advises high net worth individuals and multinational corporate groups on tax obligations arising from particular business activities or a particular type of structure. In recent years, Tania has developed a legislative drafting practice, frequently acting for His Majesty's Government of Gibraltar to produce bespoke legislation for Gibraltar in a range of areas.

Chloe Oppenheimer

Chloe joined the Corporate and Commercial team at Hassans International Law Firm in 2011 after completing her studies in the USA and UK.

Since joining the Firm, Chloe has grown her commercial practice advising a diverse client base on multinational as well as local transactions and matters. These include complex joint venture arrangements, group reorganisations, floatations on AIM, set up of local businesses, debt and equity finance deals, sale and purchase of companies, drafting legislation (most notably the Companies Act 0214) as well as data protection advice.

Chloe also advises both companies and individuals on all aspects of Gibraltar taxation. She is qualified as a solicitor in both Gibraltar and England & Wales.

Joseanne Bear

At the time of writing, Joseanne was an Associate in Hassans' Litigation department with a particular focus on commercial litigation.

During her training contract, Joseanne spent time in the Fintech team gaining experience in advising on crypto currency and blockchain related work. She also worked in the corporate and commercial department, gaining experience of corporate restructuring and the incorporation and uses of Gibraltar foundations.

Joseanne graduated from Sheffield University with a First-Class Honours in Law LLB (which included one year studying International Law at the University of Luzern in Switzerland). She subsequently completed the Bar Professional

Training Course in City University London and is a member of the Honourable Society of Middle Temple.

Joseanne has passion for travel and adventure which has seen her to the top of Base Camp Mount Everest and solo backpacking across Asia. She is also a keen scuba diver, having recently obtained her advanced open water certification.

Tessa Rosado-Standen

Tessa is a Trainee Solicitor who, prior to commencing her Training Contract, spent time as a Paralegal working closely with Grahame Jackson on tax matters in the Corporate and Commercial Department.

She graduated from the University of Cambridge with a First Class Honours in Philosophy and went on to complete the Graduate Diploma in Law. However, she then qualified as a teacher in the UK, and subsequently spent number of years living and teaching in Chile before returning to Gibraltar to resume her legal studies in parallel with raising her two small children.

Ivan Gomez

Ivan is an associate in the Corporate and Commercial Department at Hassans International Law Firm Limited, where he regularly advises on real estate development financings and other commercial ventures. He is also involved in private client matters, consisting generally of providing advice on the establishment of Gibraltar-based corporate and trust structures, which involves regularly advising on Gibraltar tax issues.

Ivan graduated from the University of Warwick with an LLB (Hons). He went on to complete the Bar Professional Training Course and thereafter undertook an LLM with a specialism in Corporate Law at City, University of London (former Inns of Court School of Law). Ivan is a member of The Honourable Society of the Middle Temple, having been admitted to the Bar of England and Wales in 2017 and enrolled as a Barrister of the Supreme Court of Gibraltar in 2019.

Caroline Lane

Caroline is an associate within the Financial Services team at Hassans International Law Firm in Gibraltar.

After graduating from the University of Reading with an LLB degree, whilst also completing a year studying Spanish law at Universidad de Salamanca, Caroline went on to complete an LLM in Corporate and Commercial Law at Queen

Mary's, University of London, before undertaking the Bar Professional Training Course at City University. Caroline is a member of the Honourable Society of the Inner Temple and was admitted to the Bar of England & Wales in 2018 and was admitted and enrolled as a Barrister of the Supreme Court of Gibraltar in 2020.

Louise Frederico

Louise Federico is a Senior Associate at Hassans International Law Firm Limited within the firm's Corporate and Commercial Department and is an integral part of the firm's gaming team.

Louise advises on a range of corporate and commercial matters, including reorganisations of international corporate structures and advising on the establishment of different corporate entities in Gibraltar. Additionally, Louise has been a key member of teams involved in multi-million-pound financing transactions.

Louise's practice focuses on gaming clients, and she has advised various gambling operators in Gibraltar in relation to licensing and regulatory matters and has been involved with the establishment of numerous operators in Gibraltar. In connection with these transactions Louise has maintained a relationship with the key stakeholders of these multinational gambling groups and has advised on their personal Private Client matters including residency, HEPSS, employment and estate planning.

Louise graduated from the University of Leeds with a 2.1 LLB (Hons) degree in law and accounting. She completed her LPC at the University of Law, London and attained the Professional Certificate of Competence in Gibraltar Law from the University of Gibraltar in 2016 and has in addition attained the Professional Certificate of Competence in Gibraltar Tax in 2019. She is a member of both the Law Society of England and Wales and the Gibraltar Roll of Solicitors.

David Montegriffo

David Montegriffo is a lawyer at Hassans International Law Firm Limited in Gibraltar and specialises in corporate law matters. David was admitted to the Bar of England & Wales in 2013 and the Gibraltar Bar in 2014. He is presently on the board of the Law Council of Gibraltar.

David acts as lead corporate counsel for high-profile clients across various industries in Gibraltar (Crypto/DLT, Gambling, Banking, Insurance). Part of his practice is also dedicated to assisting start-up companies and fledgling businesses establishing in Gibraltar and setting up their commercial operations.

David has a keen interest in local affairs and the legal and constitutional development of Gibraltar.

Isaac Avromi Endfield

Isaac Endfield is a Trainee Solicitor at Hassans International Law Firm. Isaac completed his first seat in the Tax Department working with Grahame Jackson. Isaac completed his second seat in the Corporate/Commercial Department. Isaac then moved to the Dispute Resolution Department's commercial litigation team, where he currently sits, and will soon complete his third and final seat.

In March 2020, Isaac graduated from his LLB, including a tax elective. Following his graduation, Isaac worked full-time as a paralegal. In 2022, Isaac graduated from the University of Zürich's LLM in International Business Law.

Isaac has an academic interest in tax theory particularly the tax system at the time of the Roman Empire. Outside of his professional pursuits, Isaac enjoys art galleries, racing his motorbikes, and reading about eccentrics. Isaac is also an active British Army Reservist with the Royal Gibraltar Regiment, a constituent regiment of the Queen's Division.

INDEX

Note: A detailed listing of references to legislation, international instruments and cases can be found in the Tables.